'Ventry C

Bernie Long
Bearnard Ó Lubhaing

'Ventry Calling'

Translated from the Irish by
Gabriel Fitzmaurice

MERCIER PRESS

MERCIER PRESS
Douglas Village, Cork
www.mercierpress.ie

Trade enquiries to Columba Mercier Distribution,
55a Spruce Avenue, Stillorgan Industrial Park, Blackrock, Dublin

© Translation Gabriel Fitzmaurice 2005

ISBN: 1 85635 481 4

10 9 8 7 6 5 4 3 2 1

This publication has received support from the Heritage Council under the 2005 Publications Grant Scheme

Mercier Press receives financial assistance from the Arts Council/An Chomhairle Ealaíon

This book is sold subject to the condition that it shall not, by way of trade or otherwise, be lent, resold, hired out or otherwise circulated without the publisher's prior consent in any form of binding or cover other than that in which it is published and without a similar condition being imposed on the subsequent purchaser.

Printed and Bound by J. H. Haynes & Co. Ltd, Sparkford

Contents

Translator's Note	7
Foreword	9
The Old People	11
Ventry Village *Its Background and Ecclesiastical Affairs*	21
Ventry Post Office	30
Tales out of School	39
On Land and Sea	46
The Neighbours	53
More Neighbours	71
The Feast-days of the Year	82
In Time of War	93
The Golden Age	102
The Spiddal Kid's Adventure	108
Saint Patrick's College and Dublin	114

Translator's Note

I knew Bernie Long since I returned to teach in my native Moyvane in 1975. I knew him first as an able and efficient secretary of his beloved Listowel branch of the Irish National Teachers' Organisation. I knew him later as a friend, a lover of the Irish language, a conservationist, a man who loved to talk and travel, a lover of old books, old wine and old friends. When he departed this life in August 2001, we were saddened by his death. But he had published a memoir, *Ceann Trá a hAon*, a little gem of a book, in 1998. In passing might I add that I had begged him to write, in English or in Irish, his teaching memoirs as he had a store of lore and knowledge that, alas, he took with him to the grave.

His wife, my dear friend Margery, always a staunch if not uncritical supporter of a worthy cause, did me the great honour of requesting that I translate Bernie's book. This I undertook gladly. I knew Bernie, had discussed many of the things in his book with him over the years, and was *au fait* with Bernie's outlook on the things that mattered to him. I was also *au fait* with his voice.

But how was I to translate his book? It's written in idiomatic Kerry Irish. But that is not how Bernie spoke in English. Like many of his contemporaries who grew up in the *Gaeltacht* (the Irish speaking parts of Ireland), Bernie spoke a measured and precise English. This is the voice I strove to achieve for Bernie in the following pages. I leave it up to you, dear reader, to decide if I have succeeded.

I wish to thank Aogán Ó Muircheartaigh, Pádraig Ó Fiannachta, Noel Ó Cíobháin and Pádraig Mac Fhearghusa for their interest and for their generous sharing of their time and knowledge with me. I particularly want to thank Mícheál Ó Dubhshláine for so carefully and lovingly reading, indeed editing, the manuscript and making it all the better a book in the process. I will never forget the glorious afternoon in August 2004 he took me over the Clasach (the mountain road from Dunquin to Ventry) and walked and talked me through Ventry from Saint Caitlín's Roman Catholic church to the remains of the Protestant church on the other side of the village. I also wish to thank Pádraig Ó Snodaigh of Coiscéim who originally published the book in Irish.

In publishing *Ceann Trá a hAon*, Bernie Long set down a marker for what might have followed had he been given more time. As it is, it is a loving, frank look at life as he saw it in the village of his youth, an account of his early education, and a first attempt at describing his teaching years. That in itself is valuable. I only regret that time did not permit Bernie to give us the full account of his years as a teacher, trade union activist, conservationist and *Gaeilgeoir*. *Ar dheis Dé go raibh a anam uasal.*

GABRIEL FITZMAURICE

Foreword

It is said that the human being dies twice: the first time when he dies physically, the second when he disappears from the people's memory. Most of the people I write about in this story are long dead, and before they disappear entirely from memory it is necessary to give an account of their lives. The twentieth century* is drawing to a close and like the garden at the front of my house in Killarney –

> *The days of comfort are drawing to a close,*
> *Southwards the swallow is flying*
> *And withering on its stem, the rose.*

In the days of my youth there was a silence close to mystery in the world quite unlike the noise of today. In everyday life would be heard only the whinnying of the horse, the cart squeaking on the untarred road, the dog barking, the soft plash of the oars as the currach steered for the slipway of a yellow autumn evening, the song of the hammer on the anvil from the forge near the slipway. All those sounds are silent now and in their place is the roaring of the excavator and the sharp screech of the JCB.

I was fortunate to have known that old world and like

---

* *Originally published in 1998*

everything old – old houses, old wine, old friends – it is they I value. In my writing here, I am travelling the road of memories, revisiting the familiar places of my youth, playing once again with bosom friends. We were in the springtime of our life coming of age in Ventry before we took the north road to Tralee and from there to the great, wide world. Often, as the poet said, youth is wasted on the young, but never mind. We stretched it to the full and we have no cause to complain now.

All those whose lives I write about here and have now slipped away into the shade, may their memory live among their people and may the good God shine the eternal light of Heaven on them all.

Bearnard Ó Lubhaing
The Feast of the Assumption, 1998

The Old People

My grandfather, Mícheál Ó Lubhaing, was a cooper in Ventry. He passed away in the year 1917 and with him, you could say, was the passing of the age of coopering in the westernmost part of Kerry. He learned his trade in the Isle of Man and he set up his workshop on the side of the road in Ventry.

The Ó Lubhaings hailed from Fán where they had a holding of land, and they're there still, hale and hearty, God bless them. At its peak, when the mackerel season was in its heyday in the south-western seas of Ireland and thousands of barrels of fish were exported to the United States, my grandfather had three coopers in his employ. When the demand for fish fell after the Great War there was no demand for such barrels and the cooper's trade went into decline.

My Uncle Pádraig came home from America in 1930 and attempted to make a living out of the old trade but he didn't succeed because the era of the churn and the iron barrel had arrived and the only work for the cooper was the mending of old barrels, and, even that, often without pay.

I well remember observing him working on a barrel from the bottom up, laying out the staves expertly and preparing the hoops on the anvil. There was a lot of preparation to be done with unusual implements because it was a specialised trade, the making of waterproof barrels strong enough not only to take the weight of the full barrel being rolled along the ground, but also to minimise the discharge from a frothing barrel full of whiskey or porter. All the work was done on an iron base about a square yard in extent that was laid out with great exactitude on the floor. There were three of those in the old shed where Mícheál Ó Lubhaing worked and where Pádraig was now labouring on his own. Now and then I would go back to the Poll Gorm to gather a bundle of reeds as these would be used between the staves and under the lid to keep every single drop in. I was fascinated to learn that a cooper in Burgundy employed the same invention when I visited France forty years later – again, alas, the last one of his trade left in that homeland of wine.

Poor Pádraig was forced to go into exile once again in 1933. He returned to an America that was still reeling from the effects of the Wall Street crash and the Depression. I will remember forever that day in May he left Ventry for the last time. We all knew that this was to be the leaving of no return. We were all very fond of him as he had treated us gently and generously always. He walked up the Bóthar Ard, the tears showering from him, the trunk that contained all in the world he possessed up there on the trap. He stood at the top of the road to get one last, piteous sight of his people and his native place. He died in Pittsburgh in 1938, alone in the back room that was his lodgings. He had a great love of Ireland and held out great hope that Fianna Fáil and de Valera, who were now in power, would put an end to emigration and that he would be able to return to his native place. The poor, poor man.

Talking of the old cooper, he was deeply involved in the politics of his time. He was a bitter enemy of Lord Ventry; he was a member of the Dingle Board of Guardians and also of the Congested Districts Board. He succeeded in having Lord Ventry removed from his chairmanship of the Board of Guardians, but the only reward he got for that piece of daring was to be evicted from his workshop which was then razed to the ground. Thanks to his neighbours from the whole surrounding area who came to his aid with a hundred horses and carts, the workshop was rebuilt in a single day.

He established a branch of the Land League in Ventry one morning after mass. There were two peelers present, RIC men from the barracks in the village, with their notebooks and pencils taking down evidence of the treason that was afoot. If they did, the cooper reverted to the Irish language with this advice to the peelers who hadn't a word of Irish – 'sharpen your pencil now, my boy!' He was charged on a triviality some time later in Dingle court and was sentenced to a month in Limerick prison. That is how anyone who opposed Lord Ventry in public was treated and, furthermore, he was given very little when the lands were divided, unlike those who were willing to trot after the gentry. As my brother Maidhc, always ready of speech concerning these matters, was wont to say: if the cooper wasn't such an out-and-out agitator, the Ó

'Ventry Calling'

Lubhaings wouldn't be as short of land as they are today.

The cooper was married to Margaret Knightly from Cill Mhic an Domhnaigh. They died within three weeks of each other, the story goes, as they couldn't bear to be parted. They had seven in family, but the only ones who remained in Ireland were my father, Tomás, and his sister Bridge who married Jack Shea, a carpenter, from the Holy Ground in Dingle.

My father was appointed sub post-master of Ventry in 1928, the year I was born. Prior to that, the old post office in Clochán was run by the Ó Súilleabháins, Church of Ireland people. They were of advanced age and my father had the entire running of the office for fifteen years before the old couple died.

He was a fine cut of a man, jet-black in his youth, over six feet in height and built accordingly. He was a handsome man with that Spanish complexion you often find in West Kerry, particularly in the Ó Lubhaing family. He was well educated, very fond of reading and a good man with the pen. Like many of his kind, he had no interest in farming even though he had a small-holding. Everything pertaining to farm work was left to servant-boys of whom there was no shortage – young men more than willing to work for their daily diet, a packet of Woodbines per day and five shillings on Saturday night.

He would have completed his duties in the post office, and the delivery of letters, by lunchtime. The postman's duties were discharged easily enough through the creamery and the school. Some of the outlying townlands, my father would never have seen because we, his children,

The Old People

would deliver the letters after school, and there were houses at the end of the parish who got only one letter in the round of the year – the notice demanding the rates.

On his return home, he would stretch out on the couch with a cigarette and the *Irish Press* after lunch. When he had finished smoking, he would take a *siesta* until three o'clock and then would escape to the garden where he had planted vegetables of all kinds – early potatoes and such. By night, he would 'ramble' to the cobbler's house where they would play card games – solo, whist and thirty-one to round off the day. Unlike my mother, he took life fine and easy.

He took little interest in us except to impose discipline with the leather when things got out of hand. We both feared and respected him though my mother's was the greater part when it came to rearing us and she treated us more gently than he did when we were young. That's the kind of male chauvinism that's natural to us and despite the best efforts of today's women to deny it, the whole world knows that nature is stronger than nurture.

My mother was a private kind of person who never took up 'rambling' by night or the gossip that attended it. She was too busy for that. She was a Hanafin from Lios Deargán, a small townland at the foot of Struicín outside Lispole.

In her youth she attended the domestic economy school that was set up by Lord Kenmare in Killarney to train young girls to become servants in the houses of the upper classes. There they learned the skills of cookery, needlework, lace-making, cheese-making and baking. Because of this, she was a professional cook and spent a number of years as cook in the house of a British naval captain based in Queenstown, as Cobh was called at that time.

As proof of their esteem for her, when English rule came to an end in Ireland and the captain and his household returned to Dartmouth, every so often parcels would arrive at our house containing every kind of sailors' and sporting apparel. Some of these were just the thing for our Wren costumes but my mother wouldn't hesitate to dress us for mass as little midshipmen.

As we were growing nearer the use of reason, we used to be utterly ashamed to go out in that attire, and there were often ructions in the house on Sunday mornings. But when you'd return from mass looking forward to your dinner, the morning's arguments would be forgotten in the fine smell of cooking from the kitchen. Every Sunday during the winter we had a joint of roast beef with a mouth-watering sauce, peas, Yorkshire pudding and flowery potatoes for dinner and in summer, lamb from the hill with the tang of the sea from it.

The Dingle butchers were renowned for the excellence of their meat, particularly the Moores and Currans of Green Street. There was no way my mother could be deceived in the choosing of meat as she was an expert. She would make milk pudding, or bread pudding, or steamed pudding for us every day, on Fridays maybe baked pollock with bread stuffing; steak-and-kidney pie on Saturday; delicious steak during the week and, as a special treat, doughnuts or yeast bread from time to time. While the dough was rising beside the fire, woe betide anyone who

The Old People

left the door open as the bread would be spoiled if the dough didn't rise.

Every year, she would raise a clutch of white Aylesbury ducklings for the table. When they had grown to young ducks, she would kill a pair of them on a Tuesday morning, cutting their necks with a sharp knife, making sure that the blood ran from the tops of their heads into a basin so that puddings could be made thereafter. While the ducks were still warm, she would pluck the feathers and singe the down that remained with a lighted newspaper. Then they would be hung behind the door until Saturday when she would clean them and stuff them with potatoes. When they were roasting on Sunday, the dish would be taken out every hour to baste the ducks in their own juices. What with the fragrant smell and the sight of the ducks, golden and overflowing with stuffing, we were upon them quickly. With fresh peas from the garden and new potatoes, the cuisine was up to the standard of any hotel.

Concerning my mother's family, they had a nice, comfortable farm at the foot of Struicín, sheep on the hill and the grass of eight cows. My uncle, Jim Hanafin, was married to Bridgie Kevane from Baile Liaigh in the parish of Ventry. As was common at that time, Bridgie had spent some time in America and she was a fine woman – a noble, understanding lady who never raised her voice to anybody. They had four in family along with my grandmother, Biddy Fitz from Clochán Dubh, who lived with them. I used to be sent out to pasture to them as I was growing up.

'Ventry Calling'

Life in Lios Deargán was a big change from home, there was no shop within three miles of us and all the food that was put on the table came from the farm – milk from the churn, wheat bread, buttermilk or sour milk with potatoes for dinner, bacon from the barrel or maybe a strip of kid-goat for Sunday dinner. As for the oysters, you wouldn't get the like in any but the best restaurants today. After dinner in summer we would have blackberry pie as a treat out in the garden under the apple tree. Fine, healthy food undoubtedly, but it didn't go down too well with this trickster from the post office who was used to the shop.

My grandmother was a big, imposing woman who had no time for idleness or pettishness of any kind. She had little English and, while English was spoken to the children, Irish was the language the adults spoke among themselves.

I will never forget the rosary recited every evening to complete the day. At nightfall, we would be on the ditch in front of the house waiting for the Dingle train to come puffing and whistling a mile below us as it approached Baile an Istínigh. In we'd go at twilight for the rosary and the five decades were only the beginning. Then the rubrics would start in earnest – prayers for the living and the dead, prayers for relations in America, prayers for the sick, prayers for the crops, prayers to ward off evil spirits and at long last, even as we, children, were terrified of the fairies, would come the mysterious, solemn ceremony when Biddy would rise in her long, black garb and, with the holy water, face the four corners of the house to bless them and invoke the protection of the old gods. I am convinced that this last action of hers was firmly rooted in paganism and *piseogs*, but its effect was none the less for that. Then she would rake the fire before going to sleep:

> *I rake this fire with the miraculous power that Saint Patrick received.*
> *What the angels have put together, may no enemy tear apart.*
> *May God protect our house,*
> *All that are within it,*
> *All that are without.*
> *May the sword of Christ be on the door*
> *Until the morrow's light.*

You'd sleep soundly, I can tell you, after the forces of evil had been banished and you with a mug of new milk and a crust of meal bread for supper.

As I have already said, Old Biddy was dead set against idleness, and she would keep after us during the day with every kind of chore on the farm. When she couldn't think of anything else, she would march us up the hill to gather branches in bags for the fire. The branches were thorny, unyielding and I hated the work. She would inspect the bags on our return to ensure that they were tightly packed because she discovered, once, that I had left the bottom of the bag half empty and had packed the top only. She distrusted me after that!

At the end of the holidays, the horse would be hitched to the cart on the August fair day and I would be driven to Dingle – down past Rinn Bhuí to the tarred road and along the old railway tracks that crossed the road at Baile an Istínigh, then on the old road through Gairfeanaigh

Ventry One

and down John Street of the miserable public houses where the posh restaurants are today. On meeting my own family at the Holy Ground a slight twinge of loneliness at parting from my young cousins would compete with the joy I felt at returning home. That's the world for you – the laughter and the tear.

Ventry Village
Its Background and Ecclesiastical Affairs

Even today, Ventry village in the parish of Ventry is a small and beautiful village situated snugly above historic Ventry Strand, its back to the hill and to the old high road to Dingle through Cathair Ard, Ceathrúin an Phúca, Muileann an Ghlíomaigh, Móin an Fhraoich, Cnoc na hAbha and Baile an Mhuilinn. About the middle of the nineteenth century the low road by the coast was built from Dingle to Ventry through Lord Ventry's lands, through Baile Mór, Faill na Mná and Léim an Treantaigh into the Colony. When you reach the top of Faill na Mná, you can see Ventry parish spread out before you – the fine silver strand curving to the Cuan where the fertile land is, the bogs of Baile an tSléibhe in its midst and the green, grassy fields growing sparse as you ascend the slope of Mount Eagle in the direction of the lake, Mount Eagle itself 1,696 feet in height, foretelling the weather from the western boundary of the parish. When cloud caps that mountain, bring your raincoat with you!

It was a wonderful place to grow up. The beauty of the countryside was beguiling, mysterious and the people easygoing and friendly. The earliest memory I have is of myself standing at the door of our house one Sunday morning when everybody was at mass, looking back along the

'Ventry Calling'

parish in the direction of the church. It was a fine morning in late spring, undoubtedly, the green, green fields stretching upwards to the lake, the clear blue sky above the mountains, the sweet and solemn ringing of the consecration bell sounding across the bay that was a smooth sheet of glass. Bliss was it to be alive!

On a height at the edge of the parish was a handsome, red-sandstone church built by the Irish Mission Society, Protestants who were very active proselytising in these parts from 1835 onwards. The society's school, which served also as the schoolmaster's, Master Ó Curnáin's, dwelling house, was beside the church, and below the road was the minister's house, an imposing Georgian building with its avenues, stables, coach house and gardens. Con O'Brien ran this as a hotel in the manner of *Fawlty Towers* when the mission ceased in their efforts to advance the cause of Christianity in West Kerry. All that is left of these buildings today are the foundation stones of the church and a couple of ruins where once was the rector's splendid house.

A short distance away is the little village of Ventry, more properly the Colony, two rows of small, insignificant houses built for the Protestants by the Ventry and Dingle Mission Society about the year 1835. There was a big farm that stretched all the way to Clochán to provide for the Colony with a committee to administer it. It was a sort of commune, really. In Ventry itself, 170 people had converted to the Protestant faith by 1839.

With the arrival of the Reverend Thomas Moriarty in 1839, there was an indigenous base to this movement towards conversion. Moriarty was of West Kerry stock, a graduate of Trinity College, a man of intelligence and strong personality who spoke fluent Irish. His people were well off and highly regarded in the region, though 'Tom of the Lies' was the nickname they put on Thomas himself. He established a preparatory college in Ventry for prospective ministers and those scholars would go from there to Trinity College. The preparatory college can be seen to this day, now divided into four dwelling houses stretching down from Ó Cuinn's public house; the two houses in the middle are unchanged from that time to the present.

For that reason, Ventry village was a self-contained colony about the middle of the nineteenth century. *An Cat Breac*, a little booklet used to teach simple sentences in Irish was to be found in every house. It was the aim of the Mission Society to teach Irish to the Colony and in this way the proselytisers were far in advance of the Catholic clergy in conserving and promoting the language. The movement was dubbed 'An Cat Breac' and traces of it survived up to the middle of the twentieth century.

I well remember the old folk talking about the 'Cat Breac' as if it were some kind of wild beast or a sin so grievous you couldn't speak its name out loud. There were local bible readers who read from the bible in Bedell's rich Irish to children in school and to those who were thinking about converting.

The Protestant religion had a strong footing among government officials like the RIC and the coast guard and over them all was Lord Ventry, Dayrolles de Moleyns, his steward Peter Thompson and the chief inspector of the coast guard, Lieutenant Clifford. That upper class held

'Ventry Calling'

all the power and they made sure that it was their followers got the land, the jobs and any crumbs that might fall from the rich man's table. They were no petty people in their time. There was a web of native process-servers, impounders and retainers of every kind throughout the area, faithful even to death, or nearly, to Lord Ventry in Baile an Ghóilín.

With the passage of time, between emigration, the Famine and the recovery of the Catholic Church, the movement went into decline. The school was closed and attendance at their church decreased until that, also, was closed and levelled to the ground in the 1960s. On the foundation of the Irish Free State, the rectory was bought by Con O'Brien, a former member of the RIC, and run as a hotel until the outbreak of the Second World War. Then, foolishly, he stripped the roof from that fine house so that he wouldn't have to pay rates thereby sparing himself a few paltry pounds. He sold the lead to the tinkers and he and Mary, his wife, went to live in the converted stables.

That was how it was when I was growing up, and though that era was over, the smell and the taste of the soup was still to be found over Ventry village. It was officially outside of the *fíor-Ghaeltacht* and the Dingle priests were very doubtful about it because of its Protestant background. The people who were living there were mild, agreeable people after the riots that followed the religious commotion when both sides would square up to each other and try to prove that theirs was the one true religion and that the other side had nothing but false worship, papist superstition, grasping tyrants and soupers.

Take your pick! There was no end to the swearing and cursing that would be exchanged in public and in private. Don't be talking about Christianity or Christian charity; just like in Northern Ireland in the late twentieth century, those virtues were well hidden. But now that fighting fever had died down and we were living peacefully together for the most part.

As I've already stated, the Roman Catholic Church was still very doubtful about Ventry. No priest or brother would be seen there from one end of the week to the other. Of course, they resided in Dingle and they seldom had the inclination to travel to the outskirts. As regards the people of Dunquin, when Father Tom – another Moriarty – felt it was time to bring them under Roman rule he dispatched a priest out to them, for the first time, every Saturday evening to hear confession. The less pious among them christened this attempt 'the Mission to Hong Kong!' We didn't miss the clergy. They belonged to the alien life of the big town, the life of the ten commandments – thou shalt not do this, thou shalt not do that. For that reason we didn't have any devotional life, or any demand for it, and when I went out into the world I had no inclination towards those practices.

We had one mass in the round of the week – at half past ten on Sunday morning. For a full hour beforehand, the faithful would be heading in the direction of the church that was situated in the middle of the parish. The old church stood where the school is situated now, but was moved about 1870 to distance it from the soupers and the pub.

'Ventry Calling'

Most walked to church, the odd old woman whose footing wasn't too good travelled in an ass and cart, Master Ó Curnáin with his wife and two daughters went in a trap. When those two oldsters, Maidhc Sullivan from Cathair Ard and the Masher from Cathair Bó Sine, would go by our house, my mother would say it was time for us to be on our way.

Often having fasted from midnight, we would have to wait for half an hour for the priest. On his arrival in his polished car from Dingle, a crowd would be outside, silent, bare-headed, humbling themselves before him. He would walk into the church paying no attention to the onlookers. All the women would be waiting inside the church. The mass bell would be rung and everybody would hurry inside, all except a few independent spirits who would spend their time with their shoulders to the gable of the church. Once when a rather naïve priest zoned in on an old lad who had spent most of his life mining gold in the Klondike with 'Have you any thoughts for the next world?' Klondike abruptly replied, 'One world at a time, ol' boy!'

I often recall the discrepancy that was evident every Sunday morning between the people who were reverential, in particular, and the priest with his white collar and black suit, proud and contemptuous. That's how he appeared to us, though it is likely that there was more than a touch of shyness about him also. The sermon was always in English – fine, big words in waves going over our heads, most of us not understanding a word of what was going on.

If it were Canon Lyne who happened to be there,

Ventry Village

well, he had the same rigmarole for twenty years – about the man who came on earth two thousand years ago – and most of his words were lost in the creaking of the roof of a windy day. The sermon would last forever, and we, weak from the hunger and tired of the long-windedness on the altar, would have to suffer it until my brother Maidhc would faint and two of us would have to accompany him out into the open air. That was a great relief from torment and, even if Maidhc wasn't in danger of having a weakness, we would persuade him that the fit was imminent so that we could escape.

Once a month when mass was over, the priest would come out again on the altar for the holy hour and that was an eternal penance – litanies, a couple of rosaries and prayers you'd think would never come to an end. It would be one o'clock by the time you'd get home – perished with the hunger and cold and heart-scalded by the priest and his lack of understanding.

We had to go to Dingle to be confirmed. For a couple of months beforehand, nothing but the catechism would be taught in school, and that was a scourge. This was no ordinary question-and-answer book but a cold, dry text on liturgy, ceremonies and articles of faith that was calculated to make doctors of divinity out of school children. You couldn't learn it by heart, and, anyway, we didn't understand it.

When the big day arrived, we gathered in from all the surrounding schools to Saint Mary's church, with our new suits and shining shoes waiting for the descent of the holy ghost – girls on one side, boys on the other of course. The priests would go through the seats like hawks among little birds questioning and testing us in every aspect of our understanding of the faith. The only memory I have of this inquisition is Father Tom, the old parish priest of Ballyferriter, cheerfully and in jest asking us could he use wheat bread for holy communion. This was at the beginning of the Second World War and white bread was not to be had anywhere. In fact, it was a crime punishable by prison to be caught separating wheat flour to make available smooth, white flour.

Many years afterwards I heard the real reason for Father Tom's question and, also, his merriment. It appears that Bishop Michael O'Brien had such a delicate stomach that he couldn't digest the black wheat bread the rest of us had to live on. There was a certain bakery in Kerry that used to supply white bread for the bishop's table every Friday when the bishop's emissary would arrive in his car to collect it. The police didn't know this, or maybe they did, when they raided the bakery and got evidence of this separation of flour. The owner of the bakery was to be prosecuted which would have meant jail for her and the closing down of her bakery. This same woman was a capable, versatile businesswoman and she wasn't long in letting the bishop know what her defence would be if the case went to court – that it was for the good of the bishop of Kerry's health that this illegal baking was going on. The bishop had no other choice but to go to the taoiseach, no less, Éamon de Valera, and whisper in his ear because no one else could prevent the case from being tried. The case went no further, and no wonder, but it was a private

Ventry Village

joke in the bishop's presence for that rogue from Ballyferriter on confirmation day in the church in Dingle in 1942. Father Tom was always on the side of the poor, with no airs and graces about him but a close bind with his people in the westernmost part of Kerry.

Ventry Post Office

There was only one telephone in Ventry when I was growing up and that was 'Ventry One' in the post office. It wasn't available to the public or for personal calls; it was available only for the sending and receiving of telegrams, or to send for the priest or the doctor in an emergency.

A couple of telegrams, at most, would come in the round of the week and there would be a few pennies for the delivery boy or girl. People used to be afraid of the green envelope because it brought bad news more often than not. Usually, it was my father who would go to the house if there were bad news to be broken.

I remember at the start of the war when the Japanese fleet sank the *Prince of Wales* off the Malay peninsula. That was the biggest battleship in the royal navy and both she and the *Repulse* were sunk very quickly. A telegram came from the war office in London saying that Desmond Connor, a next-door neighbour who was on the *Prince of Wales*, was 'missing believed dead'. Although my father hadn't been too friendly with the O'Connor family for twenty years on account of some boundary dispute, he wasn't found wanting when it came to informing the family and expressing his condolence. As it turned out, Desmond wasn't dead. He was rescued and spent the remainder of

Ventry Post Office

the war as a prisoner of the Japanese before returning home in 1945. But that's another story.

There was only one other telephone between Dingle and New York and that was the telephone in Dunquin. Apart from bad news, there were amusing moments on the telephone from time to time. I remember a telegram that came one day from a man who had spent a few days selling a horse at the fair of Baile an Chláir, a none too profitable venture according to the message he sent home – 'Returning home, horse unsold, porter for Martin when he gets home, expected home tomorrow'. That same man had a very high opinion of his command of the English language and on one occasion he decided to test his children on their prowess in English as he was thinking of removing them to another school that he considered to be superior. A widower, he prepared dinner for them one day; he left the pot to one side and a note on the table instructing them to 'Consume the contents of the pot'. When the children arrived home ravenous from school, they ate what was in the pot paying no attention to the father's note. When, later on, the father came home from the hill he was satisfied that they had a sufficient knowledge of English on the grounds that they had understood what he had written and he left them in the school they were in.

The mailbag would arrive every morning in a car from Dingle and, when the letters were sorted, my father would travel around the parish delivering them. The letter from America was eagerly awaited because such letters contained green dollars – a kind of Marshall Aid – and many

'Ventry Calling'

a household depended on them to pay the rates, to clothe the children, and even, at times, to put food on the table. Along with that, there was always a great welcome for the parcel from America. Because of the weight of those parcels, the people to whom they were addressed would have to come to the post office to collect them. They contained every kind of goods – silk dresses, high-heeled shoes, tobacco, multicoloured ties for the men, hats, ornaments, bracelets and many other things unfamiliar to the people back home. Size, or any such consideration, was immaterial, and if the hems of some of the dresses were sweeping the ground, or if the shoes were too big, it didn't matter. When the girls would go to the dance on Sunday night smelling sweetly of America and dressed from the skin out in silk, 'twas no help to a man in his quest for a partner if he sported an ostentatious tie from the Bronx, or Springfield Mass, or Pittsburgh as a statement of his credentials!

My mother would rise at seven in the morning in case Master Ó Loingsigh would require a stamp on his way from Dunquin to the school in Baile an Ghóilín where he taught – a journey of seven miles on his bicycle, across Mám an Chlasaigh in the depth of winter. It was I who would kindle the fire, a job I had no objection to as I had access to the sweets in the shop before anyone else would be up and about. You wouldn't have much desire for porridge, however, having filled your belly with a fistful of sweets – bull's eyes or Peggy's-legs or maybe a bar of chocolate, Half-time Jimmy.

In the course of the morning my mother would milk

the cow, tend the shop, bake bread and prepare dinner. When it was lunch time in the school, which was across the road from us, she would boil a couple of large kettles of water to fill two enamel buckets with cocoa for the pupils in wintertime. The county council made such provision for schools in the Gaeltacht – a mug of hot cocoa at midday for each child with two slices of fresh loaf spread with butter and red jam. It was the senior schoolgirls who sliced and prepared the bread and it made a fine lunch on a cold, sharp winter's day. Not even a crust would be left for the crows, unlike the sandwiches and milk that were provided by Dublin corporation which were wasted by the children of Cabra when I was teaching there in the 1950s. They turned the bottles upside down in the schoolyard, and similarly with the sandwiches.

Friday was a big day in the shop because that was the day of the old age pension – ten shillings per week and a crown for the widows.

The dole, too, was given out in the post office and those who were entitled to it had to sign their names on the form which proved difficult enough for some. I remember one man, Peaitnín, whose act of signing was performed with solemn ceremony. Firstly, a clean sheet of blotting paper would have to be placed on the counter, an ink bottle and steel pen beside it. He would savour the nib in his mouth at first and then would set about signing his name, his tongue hanging out with the effort – a big 'P' above the line, a small 'a' below and so on. This done, he would stand back to admire his work like a hen who

'Ventry Calling'

had just laid an egg, crying out 'Patrick' with the pride of his race.

If any relative of the Blasket islanders was being buried in Saint Caitlín's cemetery, the islanders would congregate in Joanie's pub after the funeral. They would walk over the Clasach on their way to the funeral and at the end of the evening most of them wouldn't be too steady on their feet. They would come to the post office in large groups requesting my mother to summon a taxi from Dingle to take them to Dunquin. The telephone was a great wonder to them – they would listen near the kiosk expecting to see the taxi man inside. There was no great welcome for them as they were reluctant to part with the price of the telephone call and you would have to watch out for them in case something would be missing after they had departed. As Séamaisín the Boiler from Dunquin once said as he was leaving Curran's public house in Dingle, the very house where Peig Sayers worked for a time as a servant-girl, with half a pig's head under his coat, 'I nearly wouldn't see you'. I am not blaming these people. They had a hard life on the very edge of Europe attempting to eke a living from the wild seas. It was no harm for them to have a slice of the action on the occasional time they came over to the mainland.

The nuns in Coláiste Íde used to invite that same Séamaisín to speak to their students so that he could communicate the wit, the elegance of speech and the rich authenticity of his accent to them. After his talk, the nuns would take him into their dining-room for a meal. Séamaisín had no great recourse to creamery butter or fresh

Ventry Post Office

meat and there was nothing he loved better than to see the mark of his teeth on the butter spread thickly on the bread. "'Tis no wonder ye have religion', he said one day to Sister Borgia as he bade farewell to the nuns who had provided him with a fine dinner and a couple of shots of whiskey for the road.

Those old timers had their own understanding of faith and morals. Monsignor Pádraig de Brún, who had a holiday home in Dunquin, was a great friend of Séamaisín. The monsignor was a scholar of Celtic Studies and Greek and was president of University College, Galway. Séamaisín was charged one time in Dingle court in relation to a bundle of willow rods that was stolen from a neighbour and the next time the monsignor came down on holiday he was teasing Séamaisín about the case. Séamaisín's riposte was concise:

> *Without rods, no panniers,*
> *Without panniers, no turf*
> *For Monsignor de Brún.*

In jest, he made a kind of accessory after the fact of the monsignor. On another occasion he was in court for having only one dog licence although he kept four dogs; he explained patiently to the judge that his animal was a bitch, that she was in heat and that that was why the other dogs were around. The judge accepted his excuse and Séamaisín left the court. While they were all in stitches laughing, he made off with the best hat among the lawyers' hats that were on the table inside the courthouse door.

'Ventry Calling'

Maybe it would be no harm to explain that the Blasket islanders didn't regulate their lives according to Roman rule. For their living, they depended on the flow of luck, from wherever it came – on the flotsam that might come in on the tide, on the low prices they would receive from the buyers of fish and likewise from cattle and sheep buyers. When they arrived on the mainland, they saw full and plenty everywhere compared to the hardship they had to endure on the island. Who would blame them if they thought they were entitled to a little of the surplus. They were simple, innocent, affectionate people, the best of company and generous with all they possessed. I was fortunate to number some of them among my friends when I grew to manhood. The pity was that they evacuated the island just as times were getting better and spent the remainder of their lives tormented with melancholy and loneliness for the Western Island.

I was in Dunquin graveyard on that cold November morning when the monument to Tomás Ó Criomhthain was unveiled. Father Tom from Ballyferriter was there to do the honours. He turned his attention publicly to Kruger Kavanagh who had got the upper hand of him in the circuit court in Tralee a few weeks previously when he was awarded his publican's licence in spite of the Church. The people of Dunquin were scattered about the graveyard – some of them, including Kruger, on the sheltered side at the gable-end of the princess' house. Behind Ó Criomhthain's grave was a rough cross, fashioned the previous night from a fragment of a box for holding oranges – two boards across each other and written on one was

Ventry Post Office

'The Poor Cóta'. The message was lost on nobody. Kruger's brother, Seán an Chóta, was the person in question and that cross was telling all and sundry that Seán an Chóta was as good a writer as Ó Criomhthain any day. The priest named out all the friends he had in Dunquin – Plate, Pound, Ceaist, the Colonel, Charlie – and then he turned on Kruger: 'I have, also, one enemy in Dunquin, but, of course, there was one scoundrel among the twelve apostles'.

Without a doubt, great enjoyment was extracted from that, but then he turned the sharp edge of his tongue on the Blasket islanders telling them straight out that the world's attention was on them while they lived on the island but now that they were scattered about the mainland they had neither respect nor recognition. It was difficult to deny it because the truth is bitter. It was the women who abandoned the island first until, at last, there was no one there but one seven-year-old boy, Gearóid Ó Cathain, and a few old people. 'The loneliest boy in the world' the English papers described him, and Michael Davitt has written a fine poem about his mother, Ceaist's wife, standing at the top of the stairs at nightfall, forever looking across the water to the deserted island.

Regarding Ventry Post Office, there are few houses in the parish today without their own telephone, and many of them surf the net to communicate across the face of the earth.

The 'islandman' is commemorated, explained, analysed and celebrated in the cathedral that is the Interpretive Centre in Béal Átha but his people had to search for a

'Ventry Calling'

slice of the action in Boston and Springfield, Massachusetts, in the New World. There's nobody at home now waiting for the parcel from America or casting an eye down the road for the postman bringing the letter with the greenbacks folded inside. They live as they please now, thanks be to God, and every day is an idle day if you so desire.

Tales out of School

There was an old fellow living above in Mám na Gaoithe and a day wouldn't pass that he wouldn't visit Ventry village. 'A little bit of heaven' he called it because there he found the pub, the shops, the craftsmen, the school and the company he loved so much. Whatever knowledge he had of heaven, we certainly had enjoyment and fun in the days of our youth, and we had variety and diversity too. First and foremost, we were bilingual. In the west of the parish, Irish was still predominant, but the villagers, by and large, had adopted English although most could speak the old tongue fluently. Nóra from the pub used to call the parishioners 'the Gaeltachts' out of contempt for the Irish language and the government's concern for them.

Ventry National School was not, strictly speaking, in the *fíor-Ghaeltacht*, the true Irish speaking area, until the middle of the 1930s when the schoolmaster made a heroic effort to remedy this situation. There were advantages – educational as well as in salary and grants – pertaining to the *fíor-Ghaeltacht*. A great number of places in teachers' training colleges was set aside for students from the Gaeltacht; post primary school grants and university grants were available to them; the teachers were paid extra. In addition to all that, there was a scheme granting £2 for shoes to any household in which Irish was the everyday language. As children, we had no interest in these affairs. There was only one other household in the village whose children were one-age to us and they spoke English, not Irish. The upshot of all this is that we spouted out English in our play after school despite the threats and abuse of the master who was trying to make true Irishmen of us!

Inspectors from the department of education would drive through the village spying on the children when we were being assessed as to our suitability for the £2 shoe grant, and any family whose children were heard speaking English was disqualified. That caused tension between the school and the village until we left school, and it left its mark on my Irish and the outlook I had on the language. That assessment caused terrible strain also, because the money for hobnailed shoes for the winter depended on it, and it was no ordinary conversation the inspector would put up with you to evaluate your fluency in Irish. I remember one small boy being questioned about what finger he would insert into the holy water font and when he didn't know, the inspector taught him a lesson on thumb, middle finger, forefinger, ring finger and little finger. If you hadn't them off by heart the next time you were questioned, you were in danger of spending the winter barefoot. Because of all this, we were inclined to favour the English language, particularly in our reading. The only books written in Irish that were available were schoolbooks; this meant that the old culture was largely hidden from us until, in my own case, I went to boarding school later on. That strain, that tension affected us greatly as youngsters. If you suspected that the master heard you speaking English after school, you would approach the schoolhouse the following morning with your heart in your boots because it would be the worse for you when you arrived there.

The schoolmaster came originally from the Machairí and was, therefore, not a native Irish speaker. He was under great pressure from every quarter to force Irish on us, so much so that he was severe, hot-tempered and often insulting. 'The Top of the Town People' he nicknamed us who came from the post office and 'The Powder Lane People' he called our good friends from the bottom of the village. I suppose he believed that he was doing his best for us and it is certain that he never spent an idle day in school. It is certain also that he made schoolteachers out of many who otherwise would have been in poor circumstances, but, in doing so, he left the mark of his handiwork, and of his hand, on us. He received the Carlisle and Blake Award, the highest award a teacher in Ireland can receive, for the excellence of his work but got little or no recognition from the locals for this remarkable achievement. If he, or any other teacher, were to achieve this distinction today trumpets would be blowing, but let it be.

The schoolmistress who taught us in the lower classes had her own problems. She was a highly unusual woman and her teaching methods were equally unusual. School inspectors were constantly harassing her because, unlike today, there was no recognition for anything that wasn't prescribed by the department. Able, intelligent teachers like her were besieged by unyielding inspectors and poisonous priests to such an extent that they grew weary of the whole business. Our schoolmistress was a wonderful woman who got great enjoyment out of the people who lived round about her. She was generous with her possessions towards anyone who was in need. Many's the five-pound-note Neilí an Chnoic and her equals got from her when times were bad and no assistance was to be had from the Irish Free State. On another occasion she gave the price of her passage to a young girl who was pregnant so that she could follow her lover over to Springfield where he had taken flight. There they married, raised their family, and returned after the war to Ireland where they lived out their days happily and contentedly.

I remember the time she threatened John Beag that she would take the pants off him if he hadn't his lessons done the following day. His father couldn't figure out why the little lad wouldn't go to school the following morning without Daddy's shirt on him!

Now and again, she would have to attend to other things besides lessons and she would post a lookout at the window in case anybody would come upon her unexpectedly. One day a lad from Cathair Ard was on duty but fell asleep and the parish priest was in the room before she had a chance to prepare for him. That gentleman from Cathair Ard woke up with a hop when the canon had departed, I can tell you.

She used to have a servant girl to do her housework but nobody could stand the hardship for too long. She sent a dispatch to her house one day requesting a stick to ram some complicated bit of knowledge into a number of

Tales out of School

forgetful scholars. A daughter of Eugene Mháire from Baile Mór was her housemaid at the time and she came up the road with the stump of a doorpost for her mistress to do the deed. On her way, she had great fun directing the attention of Morgan and the other neighbours towards what was about to happen in the school. She didn't notice that the schoolmistress was observing her play-acting from the window but on her arrival at the school with that piece of timber, she was the first to get a trouncing around the hall.

The mistress was married to a man of the same stuff as herself. He was given the name 'Frisco' and not without cause. He was a solid, stoutly built, spirited man much like James Cagney, tough in appearance but moderate in manner. He never frequented the pub and he had no regard for those who did. He was a hot-tempered man with an open disposition and if he had something to tell you, you wouldn't be long in getting an earful. 'Frisco' would regularly head off to the Pacific coast at the other side of the world when he grew tired of the climate at home.

On one occasion, his wife asked him to bring home a couple of chops from Dingle for dinner. She didn't see him again until, three years later, he strolled in the door to her and laid a parcel of chops on the table with the words 'here is your meat'. The last time he left home, the Second World War was at its fiercest on the Atlantic and there were no passenger ships travelling to America. He managed to secure a berth on a troop ship that was returning to Canada. He wrote to my father telling him his destination and requesting him to attend to certain of his affairs that he hadn't an opportunity of dealing with in the haste of his departure. He died in San Francisco at the end of the 1940s and is buried there.

A couple of years ago his grandson visited the graveyard taking with him a neighbour from Ventry who lived in San Francisco at that time and two other companions. They were trying to locate 'Frisco's' grave but had no idea where in this huge graveyard he was buried. All they knew was that his wife had a marker erected over his grave. They agreed a search plan – to spread out from the centre in all four directions. Young 'Frisco' was in charge and when he had finished speaking he felt as if the blood were draining from his body. He looked down at the ground. He was standing on his grandfather's grave.

The old national teachers were a breed apart. Many of them were learned men and women who had a great interest in folklore, in biology and in archaeology, and who had, also, a great variety of skills which they made available to the public free of charge. They surveyed land, they helped people to make their wills and to write letters, they organised all the Church collections as well as promoting the work of the Church. Many exiles from Ireland depended on the education they received in the national school, and it wasn't found wanting because accuracy and neatness were an integral part of the training they got in the reading and writing of English, in penmanship, in needlework, in knitting and in cooking, in gardening and in nature studies.

Of course, the system wasn't without fault; the slower pupils were neglected and in many cases corporal punishment was extreme and excessive. We are inclined to look back now on those days forgetting the hardship and oppression, and maybe it is just as well.

On Land and Sea

Although many of our neighbours travelled the world over and others spent time in America, many more of them hardly travelled beyond the town of Dingle in the whole of their lives. There was only one taxi in Dingle in the 1930s and not a single private car in all of Ventry parish. The priests and the doctors had cars and that was it until after the war. There was one radio set in the village (in James Curran's house) and that was heard only for the All Ireland football final; there was no electricity or sewerage system; there was no post primary education except for the few who went to the Christian Brothers' School in Dingle or to the Preparatory Colleges. But, of course, we didn't miss them, having no knowledge of them ourselves. It was understood that you occupied yourself in your spare time by using your resourcefulness and imagination and we were not lacking in those qualifications.

We were living above the sea with Ventry's white strand below us as a playing field. I believe that nobody is cut off from the wider world if he lives near the sea. We had regular contact with the continent when fishing boats from Brittany and Spain would put in to the harbour for shelter and, occasionally, to replenish their store of food and water. A great happiness would come upon us when they came ashore – wooden shoes on them, blue cotton clothes and the black berets of the fisherman. There was a strong whiff of *Gauloises* from the tobacco they rolled into cigarettes with ease and dexterity, all the while conversing in a foreign tongue.

They would exchange Spanish brandy for a sack of potatoes or loaves of bread without any interference from the custom's officer. I remember, once, the clerk came over from Ballydavid to take a quantity of brandy in bottles back to his pub with the help of my father. Needless to say, it was in the dead of night and all we, youngsters, knew about it was what we learned from eavesdropping on the whispers the following morning. The clerk was my mother's cousin and, but for that, he wouldn't have obtained any help in our house for his mischief as she saw it.

With the ebbing and flowing of the tide twice a day, the view of the countryside by the sea is constantly changing. When the tide went out, leaving pools among the rocks, we could examine closely the world beneath the waves. In these pools we sailed our boats – little boats we made at home from a thick piece of wood, the hole for the mast burned out with a spike we reddened in the fire, a piece of a rag for a sail. The now-disused cooper's tools were very handy for this undertaking. If war broke out on the 'sea', there would be no shortage of shells for the battle, stones would be showered on the enemy's fleet, bombs exploding in every direction such was our zeal. We were much influenced by the First World War and the bloody battles in the trenches – stories that somehow spread from mouth to mouth. From their reading, that gentle boy, Eoin Curran, and my brother Maidhc were experts in these matters

'Ventry Calling'

and we would re-enact the battles of the western front on the rocks east of Tobar na hAille. Periwinkles were soldiers, heights and hollows and rock pools were trenches; we had small stones for the deadly bombing, and after the carnage and destruction we wreaked upon the periwinkles, you could imagine the battlefields of Passchendaele or Flanders after the slaughter.

We would go back the strand for more realistic battles. We re-created the trenches by digging the sand with shovels, and, with sods of turf as munitions, we bombarded each other with vigour. This turf was plentiful when the tide was out because, according to folk memory, it was originally bogland that was now eaten into by the sea. We wouldn't think twice about using stones from time to time if turf was in short supply and the battle was raging. When my brother's head was split during one of these battles, necessitating the attention of the doctor for a stitch, that put an end to such realism. At the same time, however, we conducted many an ambush on innocent people, bombarding them with clods.

We were very much taken by the deeds of Tom Barry and his exploits in West Cork. We were able to make harmless bombs by putting some grains of carbide into cocoa tins with a hole punched in the bottom. After a few minutes, when the tin would be filled with gas, if you put a lighted match to the hole, there would be a noisy explosion that would blow the cover off with such force that anybody cycling by would think, at least, that the tyre of their bicycle was punctured. Carbine was used by the police, and also by my father at that time to provide light for bicycle lamps and we had easy access to it.

When the Fitups came with the first movies, and the comics arrived in parcels from America, we became acquainted with cowboys and Indians. With the help of Zane Grey's stories, the sandy ground as prairie and six-guns from Maggie Devane's shop in Dingle, we were rigged-out to spend the day as *Riders of the Purple Sage* or to chase Apaches or the Cherokee among the sand dunes.

From November to May there was no fine Sunday that we wouldn't be on the hill hunting the hare or the fox with greyhounds and other dogs of indeterminate breed. Now and then in the springtime the dry furze would be set on fire and there would be the drive to keep the fire under control – flames and smoke and heat driving us back.

Once a year we would visit the top of Mount Eagle that was in front of our house to the west like an Everest or a Kilimanjaro. Mount Eagle was our weather forecast – if it was clear, the weather would be fine, but it was more often scowling down on us through cloud and fog. It was there in full view until the sun would go down behind it, a mysterious, magical place and it was a big day in our lives when we managed to break its secret.

On a fine Sunday in midsummer we would set about climbing it, up Cill a' Ruith, along by the lake and the cliff behind it to the soft, smooth top where turf was cut. The first time I saw that lake in the mountain recess, it both amazed and terrified me – it was dark and mysterious, and a lot bigger than one would have thought. From the top of the mountain was a boundless sight, stretching

'Ventry Calling'

out over the wide sea, steam boats on the horizon, the Great Skellig and Valentia Island and the Iveragh peninsula to the south, and to the north, the Shannon estuary. We were no different to the little boy from the Great Blasket who cried that Ireland was long and wide when he saw the same sight from the top of the Clasach on his way to the Ventry races.

We would regularly go to Leaba an Fhir Mhuimhnigh – a dolmen in the mountains above Cathair Ard; another day to Tuirín Bán in Baile an Ghóilín near the mouth of Dingle harbour; another day would be set aside for Cé an Chuain and the ruins of the coastguard station that was burned down during the War of Independence; and every Easter Sunday we would journey to Teampall Mhancháin in Baile Riabhach to visit the holy well for the pattern. We were feeling our way on foot to the borders of our own small world, our understanding of our history expanding accordingly.

We played football enthusiastically on the sandy ground behind the dance hall, and we had to retrieve the ball from a bog hole or a furze bush more than anything else.

In fine weather we would go swimming from the slip to the strand; sometimes, depending on the tide, to Cé an Bháid; and, when we got older, to Poll na gCaorach where there was always a depth of water. We were like seals, bucknaked and belly-to-sun, until Mrs McDonnell complained. She couldn't go gathering sea-grass without facing Dinny Sugrue and his sons along with him, and we all giving scandal to the neighbourhood! God between us and all harm!

On Land and Sea

During the summer, also, we would often spend a chunk of a day fishing for wrasse from the rock below Faill na Mná, limpets as bait, our fishing rods made of bamboo from Baile an Ghóilín. There was great satisfaction to be had from this fishing when the tide would be coming in and the wrasse biting greedily. There was great demand for this coarse fish which was salted in barrels for the winter.

When the weather was fine, it was lovely to walk on the beach with your bucket to be filled with the gatherings of the seashore, as it was called. You would have periwinkles, scallops, dilisk, carrageen moss, crabs, mussels and countless shellfish, for which we had no names, in your bucket going home. There was a big bed of shellfish in Cuas na Feamnaí, but, because they had a reputation for causing diarrhoea, almost nobody would take the risk but the odd toper who had a craving for them.

All in all, it is difficult to imagine how anybody would die of the hunger with the abundance of food that was under our feet. In the folklore of the people, however, this abundance was so caught up in their minds with the bad times that they had a very poor opinion of that food, especially the small farmers. Nowadays, the gleanings of the seashore are among the most delicious, and most expensive, dishes in the upmarket restaurants in Dingle.

In the depths of winter, we would retreat to Curran's kitchen which I have already mentioned. On such nights, there would be a big fire of timber from the woods in Baile an Ghóilín lighting in the open grate. There was a big table made of pitch pine which was washed up on the tide and it is on that we played our quarrelsome games of cards, ludo and chess. Mícheál Curran and his wife, Nóirín, were friendly and welcoming – there were no strict rules and we were free from the discipline imposed on us at home. There was no prohibition on smoking tobacco, and it is there we became acquainted first with girls.

Mrs Curran was a lovely lady in mind and personality, a farmer's daughter from East Limerick, the fertile plain of Munster. Like many people from that side of the country, she had a great love for Irish traditional music and dance, and she tried hard to teach us the dance steps to the music of the concertina. In that house were books that related to the grandfather, Master Curran, and these were shared generously. In the Ireland of that time, it was the lack of books that most distressed me. It was in that house I first became acquainted with *Coral Island, Treasure Island, The Magic Wand,* the *Just William* stories, Kickham and many others who whetted an appetite for literature that has been a support to me ever since. I will be forever indebted to the Currans for the pleasure, the fun and the education we got in that warm, cosy back-kitchen in the days of our youth.

The Neighbours

The small village at the top of the beach was a microcosm of the history from which we sprang. To the person who didn't understand our culture, it was only an insignificant village. There was a religious and linguistic diversity there that greatly added to its personality. We had contact with the seagoing cultures of France and Spain and with our own culture whose remains were visible all around us.

Behind in Fán on a little piece of land high above the sea was Dún Beag – an old *dún*, or fortification, that was built on top of the cliff by the first settlers in Ireland four thousand years BC.

Once when my father was digging in his garden, his spade fell from his hand into an underground chamber that lay hidden for a thousand years. When the entrance was cleared, the archaeologists were able to enter the chamber without hindrance to examine it. It was a souterrain and it was so well made that, even after all those years, there wasn't a trace of dampness. You would have to crawl into it on your belly, a thing we often did, and inside was a round room in which you could stand. The floor was covered with the shells of cockles and limpets – the remains of the last meal that was consumed there. In the neighbourhood of my father's garden in Clochán, there is a maze of underground caves which proves that, like in

'Ventry Calling'

Cro-Magnon in France, people were living here in prehistoric times.

It is evident from these remains that are spread throughout the district, hundreds on the southern flagstones of Mount Eagle alone, that humans have been living here continuously for more than four thousand years. This leaves its impression on the people and on the land. It gives substance and self-confidence to the old people who are firmly grounded in the old culture and in pagan times because their roots go back to before the coming of Christianity. In their background was the story of the first, prehistoric invasions, the Megalithic Age, the pre-Christian Age, the Age of Christianity, the Vikings, the Normans, and, in the end, the change of religion and the English.

When I was growing old enough to fend for myself, the Free State was being helped to its feet and a great effort was made to conserve the Irish language, but, even so, we had a close relationship with England and the empire. We had a poor opinion of the goods that were beginning to be manufactured in Irish factories, considering them to be inferior and roughly made compared to anything 'Made in Birmingham' or Coventry or Manchester. The view was taken that anything that came from England, whether person or thing, was vastly superior to its counterpart in Ireland – to anything that carried the words *Déanta in Éirinn* ('Made in Ireland').

The youth, of course, were under the influence of a history devised by the Christian Brothers – the Fianna, the Island of Saints and Scholars, the Penal Laws and the

The Neighbours

War of Independence – so that we were very uncertain about our new situation and our ability to establish a new republic. We were influenced by the *Wolfe Tone Annual*, published by Brian Ó hUiginn in the 1930s, which was brimming over with the propaganda of this new age – ballads, articles, accounts of the heroes of the Easter Rising and the War of Independence inciting our nationalistic opinions. The *Irish Press* was founded and it was our gospel of the day – 'do chum Glóire Dé agus onóra na hÉireann' ('for the Glory of God and the honour of Ireland'). De Valera and the pope were in regular competition for the front page, but we were more interested in *Captain Mac*, *Roddy the Rover* and *Mickey Mouse* on the back page. We had books like *Tragedies of Kerry* and the *Jail Journal* to fan our hatred of the Free Staters and the English who, in any case, appeared to us as one and the same. In that way, we were much under the influence of our history and our culture, whether they were true or false.

For a small village, Ventry supplied most of the requirements of the times, and these were few. There were three blacksmiths, a shoemaker, a tailor, a dressmaker, a carpenter, a cooper, fishermen and farmers working there, and a post office, a pub, three shops and a dance hall. The same were to be had in every village in Ireland but, in my opinion, the people we grew up among in Ventry had personality above the usual along with independence both of mind and of religious belief.

At the top of the village was the post office and below it was a row of four houses, the first of which was Joanie's pub. This row of houses was formerly the Preparatory College established by Reverend Thomas Moriarty, 'Tom of the Lies', for Protestant students. Joanie was a widow who had her son Morgan and daughter Nora living with her. Neither of them married as a result of which they both spent their lives casting aspersions on everybody. You were damned if you frequented the pub too much, and even more so if you didn't go in at all. There was a hereditary enmity between the Flahertys and the Ó Lubhaings. In the old days they used to throw insults at each other over the ditch – 'Coopereen the firkins', 'Draineen the bottles' – and things didn't improve in my time. Both women detested being called by the names 'Joanie' or 'Nonie' even though the pub was widely known as 'Joanie's Pub'. One verse went thus:

> *I travelled Cork and sweet New York,*
> *And Dublin town all over,*
> *But I never tasted a sweeter drop*
> *Than Joanie Manning's porter.*

I remember when Muiris Ó Súilleabháin's fine book, *Fiche Bliain ag Fás*, was published; in it he gave a hilarious account of the visit he and his friend Tomás Eoin Bháin paid to the Ventry Races. They ventured in to the pub and, though only young boys, they called for two pints of porter which they got without a question being asked. That didn't trouble the Flahertys: what did trouble them was the disparaging account Muiris gave of the old woman who served them. They were twenty years waiting for satisfaction. Nowadays, Ó Súilleabháin would be in the high court for libel but for the Flahertys it was sufficient that they got the opportunity to give him a tongue-lash-

The Neighbours

ing when, many years after the book's publication, he called into their pub for a pint. From that day on, poor Muiris couldn't call into Joanie's to quench his thirst. Nora was a clever, handsome girl in her youth, but, like many more, nobody was good enough for her and she let her life go to waste.

Nora's father, John Flaherty, was a schoolmaster. He came from the Machairí and died suddenly when his children were young which left a large void in their lives. Nora was well educated and had a fine collection of old books, Foley's *History of Ireland*, *Romantic Hidden Kerry* and many others, that she used to lend to me. The sharpness of her tongue wasn't blunted with the passing of the years. It was the one defence she had against drunkards who came in to the pub, particularly on fair day evenings, to continue their squabbling and they often without the price of a pint after a bad day at the fair. On the other hand, she got great pleasure from talking to educated people, visitors to the area and the like.

Concerning Morgan, he always had money to draw on and it is unlikely that he ever did a day's work in his life. He was a small man who was always mocking people, but he had humour to the marrow of his bones. Although he drank nothing but sherry, he managed to drink his fill unknown to his mother and Nora who thought that he never touched a drop. Although they never wanted for anything, or suffered any hardship, Nora and Morgan lived a miserable, lonely life. They never wronged anybody and that's no small achievement for any person, alive or dead.

Below the pub was Ó Conchúir's little shop – a cor-

'Ventry Calling'

rugated iron structure added on to the front of the dwelling house with a big yellow AA sign over the door announcing that it was one hundred and ninety-six and a half miles to Dublin! Mrs Ó Conchúir's shop was for children only with every kind of sweet, bar and toy on sale there. The shop window could have been out of *Coronation Street* with its picture of the king of England as centrepiece. Also in the window were moneyballs, Liquorice Allsorts, liquorice pipes, lucky bags, blackjack and none of them cost more than a halfpenny. If you went in to Mrs Ó Conchúir with a penny, you would get a moneyball – with maybe a halfpenny hidden inside – and a generous fistful of sweets in a cone-shaped twist of paper. She spent her youth working in the house of some nobleman in England and she was as loyal to the king as anybody in the kingdom. Her husband, James, was a former petty officer in the royal navy and he was so spick-and-span-military that he would put you in mind of nothing else but the 'chief petty officer' who spent twenty years and a world war in the royal navy. When he walked out in the morning, shining black gaiters over his sailor's boots, a staff under his oxter, even though he was going only to the cow-house, you would think he was on board a battleship inspecting the parade. Johnny Hick nicknamed him 'Sir James Craig' and his wife 'Lady Evergreen'. Johnny had a nickname on everybody in the village, and, somehow, you couldn't imagine them having any other name. Mrs Ó Conchúir would be up and about at seven o'clock in the morning busily beating mats against the ditch in front of her house, cleaning and scrubbing as if she, too, were in

The Neighbours

the navy. Cleanliness (of her person and her house) was the most important thing in life to her after her only child, Desmond, to whom I have already referred [p. 30]. Desmond was not permitted to have any contact with the neighbours for fear it would interfere with the ideal she had for him – a kind of Little Lord Fauntleroy. No wonder he was sent to the naval training college in Portsmouth, and that is how he came to be swimming for his life off the Malay peninsula in 1941. He came home from the prisoner of war camp in 1945 an out-and-out alcoholic. His mother died of a broken heart a few years afterwards and it tested Desmond and his father not to fall into her grave on the day of her funeral with the dint of drink. Desmond returned to England and nothing was heard of him thereafter.

Below 'Craig's' shop lived another former sailor, John Kevane, a widower with three children, a pleasant, jovial man. When his wife died, the grandmother, Bríde Bhán, took the youngest girl, Gretta, into her thatched cabin on the side of the road; and when John himself died shortly afterwards, Maggie Knightly, a dressmaker who was a cripple, took the two other orphans, Máirín and Jóin, in until they were grown up. They both had sweet singing voices and when they sang each other to sleep at night it would remind you of the tragic story of the children of Lir. Their uncle, Peaitnín Griffin, the man who dispensed the dole, and his father, the carpenter, lived in that house until they died. Their only wealth in life was a crab-apple tree at the back of the house that never came to ripeness. Because it was the only apple tree in the neighbourhood, it was in great demand among apple-hungry children.

A certain man used to have his own use for it when he went courting a French-Canadian woman who came to live among us during the war. While the neighbours were at mass, he would sneak across the green, a small satchel of crab apples as a love offering, and we have no reason not to believe that there was a welcome for him and his apples. She was married to a man from Paróiste Múrach who was drowned when a German torpedo sent the ship, the *Kerry Head,* to the bottom of the sea. The *Kerry Head* belonged to the old Limerick Steamship Company and sailed dangerous seas during the war in an attempt to keep us alive with cargoes of food and other goods from foreign lands. Often, the Germans made no distinction between Irish shipping and the enemy. She went down with all hands in under three minutes. The woman from Canada had three children: the oldest boy, Gordon, was black; the second boy was pure French in appearance; and there was no doubt but that the girl was the daughter of the man from Paróiste Múrach. Shortly after he was drowned, his wife hoisted her sails for Limerick city where she had more scope to ply her trade.

Master Curran lived in the last house in College Row, and he built a fine, three-storey edifice beside it that operated as a hotel in our time. James Curran and his sister, Nóra, lived in the old house and they ran the hotel. Many famous people, from Cecil French Salkeld to Seán Ó Faoláin, stayed there before the war. Years afterwards, when Beatrice, Salkeld's daughter, married Brendan Behan, they paid a visit to Joanie's pub one day. Late in the even-

The Neighbours

ing, Nóra remonstrated with Brendan on the grounds that he had drunk too much and wasn't paying his wife sufficient attention. Behan said, in his defence, that Beatrice's father was an old alcoholic, and that Beatrice was well accustomed to the ways of drink. 'If that is so,' replied Nóra, 'he was always a gentleman, not like the scoundrel who married his daughter'.

Another one of the Curran family, Annie, was married to Donnchadh Ó Siochrú, a brother of An Seabhac, the famous writer from Baile an Ghóilín. Donnchadh, in his youth, was a policeman in London at the time of Michael Collins. When the War of Independence broke out, he was Collins' go-between with the underground in London who were attempting to provide arms and munitions for the volunteers. Annie would go shopping to Covent Garden with her infant son, Kevin, in his pram where a parcel of guns and bullets would be placed under the infant along with the vegetables.

Collins sent over two volunteers from Dublin to kill a detective from West Kerry who had risen in the ranks of Scotland Yard. He was suspected of having been involved in the capture of Roger Casement in 1916 because it was he who was sent over from England to accompany Casement from prison in Ireland to Pentonville prison. When Annie Curran learned about the mischief that was afoot, she sent a message to the detective's wife, who was born in the same area as herself, so that the attempt failed.

Annie was a brave, big-hearted woman who was more concerned for the well-being of her neighbours than the aims of the war that was being conducted without mercy

'Ventry Calling'

on every side. When the Treaty was signed in 1921, Donnchadh and his family returned to Ireland where he was appointed a sergeant of the garda síochána, the new police force, without delay. The whole family used to come to Ventry from Galway every summer and the young Ó Siochrús greatly added to our youthful frolics as they were spirited and clever in their company and in their minds, traits they inherited from their family. When Donnchadh came out on pension from the police, he and Annie returned to Ventry where they spent the rest of their lives in the one house with James and Nóra.

Above the strand was Ó Cíobháin's house, which still stands. There old Thady kept his shop, a bearded man whose wife was dead. It was a big, spacious house with rooms that were let to guests. It is there that Eveleen Nicholls, who was engaged to be married to Patrick Pearse, if we can believe the story, lodged before she went out to the Great Blasket where she drowned tragically in 1909. In the shop was a box packed with dates from Egypt for which there was great demand although they were stuck together in a hard, stiff block.

When he died, Tadhg, Thady's son, took over, an erudite, intelligent man whose interest in literature was far greater than his concern for the shop. He was reluctant to leave down his book to serve a customer and he preferred by far to discuss Social Credit or Muintir na Tíre than to go on about football. One day, a man from Dublin called in to the shop enquiring the way to the Great Blasket and Tadhg admitted in the course of conversation that he had never set foot on the island. The Jackeen said that that

The Neighbours

was a great shame for him. After a moment's reflection, Tadhg enquired of the Dubliner if he had ever been to the top of Nelson's Pillar. The Dubliner had to admit that he hadn't. 'Well, I have', countered Tadhg. *Touché*.

A short distance down the road from the Ó Cíobháin dwelling was a gorgeous little thatched house where lived John McNamara from Miltown Malbay, a former member of the Royal Irish Constabulary, who was married to Caitlín Ní Shé, a schoolmistress from Cill Mhic an Domhnaigh. It was a veritable doll's house and not a trace of it remains today. Right beside it was, and still remains, a wooden bungalow built by The O'Rahilly in 1912 for his wife, Madame O'Rahilly and their young family. The O'Rahilly was born into the world as Michael Rahilly, the only son of Richard Rahilly, a wealthy shopkeeper from Ballylongford and a loyal subject of the empire. His son was educated in Clongowes Wood College and in the Royal University of Ireland but he didn't succeed in obtaining a degree. He was only seventeen years old when he met Nancy Browne, a young girl from Philadelphia, who was holidaying in Ireland with her mother and four sisters.

Mrs Browne was a wealthy widow whose family had woollen mills in Philadelphia and lived on Fifth Avenue. Michael Rahilly and Nancy Browne were married in New York in 1899 and returned to Ireland ten years afterwards. They bought a house, 40 Herbert Park, in Ballsbridge in Dublin and that was their residence. He became involved with the political movements of the time, he appropriated to himself the old Gaelic title, The O'Rahilly, and spent summer after summer in Ventry. It is there that he met Desmond Fitzgerald who was living nearby in Cuan at that time, and Ernest Blythe, a member of the Church of Ireland from south County Antrim, who came to work as a servant boy in a farmer's house in Minard. All three shared the same aim – to learn Irish as a foundation to the nationalism they were proclaiming. It is clear from Fitzgerald's memoirs that a large part of the plans for the Easter Rising were discussed in that bungalow in Ventry and on the walks they had on historic Ventry beach. Even though The O'Rahilly was completely opposed to Pearse's strategy for the Rising, and strongly in favour of Eoin MacNeill, he didn't fail his men when the Rising went ahead. The O'Rahilly's conduct during Easter Week 1916 was of a piece with Marshal Ney in Napoleon's army – he was 'the bravest of the brave'. At the end of the week, he was mortally wounded leading his men on an escape route down Moore Street. He was twenty hours lying on the side of the street before he died. Madame O'Rahilly was noble and proud of mind and in appearance – at a remove from politicians and with little respect for them. Every year for the rest of her life, she and her five sons came on holiday to Ventry where they were held in the highest esteem and affection, particularly the youngest son, Ruairí, who was born after his father's death. Ruairí contracted polio in his youth as a result of which one of his legs was so wasted that he had to wear a special shoe and metal callipers to support his leg. He never yielded to this affliction and he took an active part in every game when he was growing up. The bungalow is still owned by The O'Rahilly's near family and, even though it is a wooden edifice, neither damp nor

The Neighbours

the passage of years has done it any damage. It remains as firm and strong as the indomitable mind of the man who built it more than eighty years ago.

I have already mentioned the rector's old house at the edge of the village that was converted into a hotel by Con O'Brien. Visitors to the area were scarce in the 1930s and Con began to hold dances in the cellar. The clergy were totally opposed to these dances and Con and the priests of Dingle fell out bitterly on that account. In Sunday sermons, the dances were consigned to the furthest reaches of hell and Con, and anyone who frequented those dances, was charged with mortal sin. When his Christmas dues weren't forthcoming, Canon Browne proclaimed one Sunday morning: 'Mr and Mrs O'Brien – nil; they are, of course, old defaulters of mine but their money will melt like the froth on the river'. It was a great injustice to inoffensive people who were depending on the few shillings they got from providing a place where the youth could dance a couple of sets on a Sunday night.

It was mainly visitors from England who patronised the hotel and there was no fear that they would ever return, or even spend the full term of their reservation there. For instance, one gentleman came to spend a fortnight's fishing in the area; he didn't turn up for breakfast on his first morning in the hotel and Nell Russell, who was waitressing, went to search for him. There was no sound from his bedroom, only a mysterious silence, and, in the end, she opened the room door discreetly. The ceiling had fallen on the bed during the night and the visitor had vanished without trace.

'Ventry Calling'

The food was of a standard with everything else – anything could happen. There was a deep well in the middle of the yard and it was usually left uncovered. Once a clutch of young ducks fell in and drowned. Connie was short of victuals to cook for dinner and he asked the serving girls to pluck the ducks, a thing they couldn't do because, being young ducks, they were covered in down. Connie got a tin of paraffin and set fire to the down. The guests thought they were dining on crow that evening!

On another occasion, Nell was waiting at the front door in her white apron and lace cap to welcome two upper class English women who had arrived while Con was at the back of the hotel attending to a young sow and a litter of piglets. The sow and the piglets broke out and advanced with fury around the corner of the hotel towards the two gentlewomen who were just then alighting from their motorcar. Talk of commotion – women and piglets screeching, Con frothing and foaming and Nell between laughter and tears! There was no danger that Somerville and Ross would ever have to invent such stories while the like of Con was at large!

Up the laneway was a fine farmer's house that belonged to the Hicks. The Hicks were of Palatine stock and there was no end to the mixture of culture, religion and high jinks in that house. When Joe Hick married Máire Mhóráin, a Catholic, he converted to Catholicism for the occasion. The moment of truth came the following Sunday when he and Máire came to the end of the laneway. 'I wonder will I go east or west' he exclaimed. He went east to his own church as his family had always done and Máire wasn't too worried about which church she would attend. You might say that they had a foot in both camps; they paid little heed to the *Ne Temere* decree as they raised their children as honest Protestants.

The Hicks were the best of neighbours and kept an open, welcoming house at all times. The commotion and strife that goes on in every household, and that many people try to keep to themselves, were on public display in Hick's. None of them was anxious to leave the old abode to allow the one who was to inherit the farm marry, and, for that reason, they often quarrelled among themselves. In the middle of all the commotion Billy or Jack would announce that he was going to America and he would bid them all a sad farewell. He would walk down one laneway and up the other one immediately afterwards. On his return, he would be asked what time he arrived in America and the racket would begin all over again. They were simple people without any malice, whose sense of humour was always to the fore.

When a new minister arrived at their house, once, from Northern Ireland, an out-and-out Orangeman who thought that the Protestants were too friendly with the Catholics, Johnny got rid of him by saying bluntly that it is by mutual assistance that people live. The only problem was that the Church of Rome was proclaiming that it was necessary for everybody to belong to the Catholic Church and that there was no salvation to be had outside it.

The Catholic clergy forbade us to go into the Protestant church even on the day of a wedding or funeral. It was a disgraceful thing to do. They could not, however, prevent us from going to wakes, and a wake in Hick's house was as good as a wedding any day. It would go on for two days and two nights and there were pipes of tobacco, porter and snuff aplenty. It was there we got our first taste of alcoholic drink and our first puff of tobacco, and, because it was in honour of the deceased, they greatly pleased us.

There was both friendship and respect between the two religions in Ventry, despite memories of the religious wrangling of the nineteenth century. I remember one man, 'Cotter' as he was called though his real name was Ó Muircheartaigh, a sturdy, bearded man given to drinking and dissipation, who made use of both sides as it suited him. I suppose it was the last relic of the old religious dispute that was still nurtured by the clergy. Cotter was raised a Protestant but was known to turn Catholic when he thought it would go better for him depending on which way the wind was blowing. Spiritual matters didn't count on even the biggest bead of his rosary, not that he had any use for a rosary no matter which side was in fashion. Priest and parson went to war over Cotter's soul. No week went by that he wasn't visited by one or other with a half-quarter of Bendigo tobacco and noggins of whiskey. He lived in a house provided for him by Bean Uí Mhuircheartaigh, the schoolmistress. She repaired that old ruin of a house in the Colony with money and devotion and installed Cotter there so that, having nothing to trouble him, he couldn't care less who made the world.

All in all, the Protestants were decent, likeable people

The Neighbours

whose gentility and honesty were far greater than some of the 'true Gaels'. Their standards, their fidelity to their own faith and their Christian living was an example to the whole community. It is a pity that their numbers have declined. As I have already mentioned, the Ó Súilleabháins had the old post office in Ventry. They came over from the Great Blasket after they converted from Catholicism. Two of their family were ordained as Protestant ministers and one of them spent a time in New Zealand. I remember the newspapers he used to send to Mártan and Johanna, his last two remaining relatives at home. He advanced in his Church until he was made dean of Saint Paul's in London. The other man won high recognition, also, in the Church of his choosing when he was made bishop of Tuam. The Blasket islanders had great powers of recovery when they threw off their fetters!

There is a remarkable chapter in local history about Canon James Goodman who lived from 1826 to 1896. The Goodman family lived in Baile Mór and were connected with the Protestant ministry in Dingle throughout most of the nineteenth century. They were highly respected and greatly liked because of their generosity, their nobility and their sympathy with the old Irish culture. James Goodman spent the early years of his ministry, from 1860 to 1866, in Ardgroom in the Beara peninsula, and, while he was there, Tomás Ó Cinnéide, the famous piper from Ventry, used to visit him for long periods. The Ó Cinnéide house was still standing in my time in Ventry; it stood just on the east side of the Protestant church. Goodman was a musician and a Gaelic scholar and he took

'Ventry Calling'

down more than 700 tunes from Ó Cinnéide. This fine collection is to be seen in four manuscripts now in Trinity College, thanks to the blind piper from Ventry and the rector from Baile Aimín. By coincidence, the first volume of two volumes of this wonderful store of music gathered by Goodman has been edited by Dr Hugh Shields and published as *Tunes of the Munster Pipers* by Taisce Cheol Dúchais na hÉireann.

Goodman had a great friendship, too, with Pádraig de Lóndra, another musician from Ventry who, among many other tunes, gave him the beguiling air 'An Buachaill Caol Dubh'. It is worth mentioning in this context that there is a limestone arch in front of his church in Skibbereen in honour of Canon Goodman, scholar, neighbour and Gael.

As W. B. Yeats said 'We are no petty people'; their decline is a great loss to Ireland and we will not see their likes again any more than the Blasket islanders that Ó Criomhthain lamented long ago.

More Neighbours

Down at the bottom of the village was the old RIC barracks, a well constructed building over the sea, a sunny chamber sheltering the front door which was always freshly painted blue. This was Ó Muircheartaigh's house. One of that family, Tommy, joined the British merchant navy at the start of the war having qualified as a radio officer in the Marconi College in Wales. He survived the war even though many times he sailed on the brink of eternity in the convoys across the Atlantic and north to Murmansk on the edge of the Arctic ocean.

When he came home on leave, his stories about the war at sea were better than any television programme you'd see today. He was a fine storyteller. We sailed with him to Newfoundland and Toronto, across the South Atlantic to Buenos Aires and Montevideo and north to the dangerous North Sea with cargoes of munitions for the Russians. After the fall of France, he helped to rescue a part of their fleet for the allies when they sailed from Marseilles to Algeria. He pointed out to us that it was no disgrace to soil you pants with fear when a Messerschmitt came unexpectedly out of the fog on the Norway coast, bullets making bits of the wireless cabin where you were trying to send mayday calls across the airwaves. After the war he was sent to Pakistan as a chief representative of Mar-

'Ventry Calling'

coni. Having spent a few years there, he returned to Wales as instructor in charge of the Marconi Training College. However, the wanderlust came upon him after a while and he resigned his post to sail on a whaling ship out of Capetown. He died suddenly of a heart attack on board the whaler in the Antarctic.

His body was brought back to Ireland, having been kept under ice until they returned to Capetown. That's how he would have wanted it, a versatile, spirited rover who left us the better for having known him and his exploits. He was a crucial part of our education. Even though he wasn't a day older than two score years when he died, he had done so much and seen so much in those years as wouldn't be achieved in three ordinary lives.

Down in the Colony lived Maidhc McDonnell and his wife, Bridgie Ferriter, who taught school in Cill Mhic an Domhnaigh. Maidhc was Bridgie's faithful servant. He returned from America, an accomplished mechanic, he bought a Model T Ford and married Bridgie who was many years his senior. It was a lot easier than returning to the depression in America.

He had a fine garden on the edge of the cliff and in it he grew every kind of crop. He had early potatoes for dinner before the others would have sown theirs. He had a currach which he named *An Madarua* (*The Fox*) on the slipway, so named to refute the old superstition of the fishermen. If you called out 'madarua' after them as they were putting out to sea, they would have no luck. The *Madarua* didn't ever do much fishing – the people of Baile Mór used to opine that it was a great sign of the weather when the Ventry currachs put out to sea. Maidhc and Bill Rooney had a couple of lobster pots, a trammel-net to catch a variety of fish in the flowing tide, trawl-lines to catch stray mackerel, and new-fangled feathers for pollock.

The food on Maidhc's and Bridgie's table was the equal of anything in Benner's Hotel in Dingle – the finest fruits of garden and of sea. Maidhc was resourceful and youthful in outlook with a great understanding for young people. It was a pity that Maidhc and Bridgie had no children of their own.

In the Colony, too, lived the Brownes, most of whom joined the British forces – one way or another. Bessie, the old woman, was a Protestant schoolmistress. One day when her son Nicholas was coming in her way at home, she dealt him a blow of a brush on the back and cleared him out the door. He didn't stop running until he reached the coastguard station at the harbour across the strand where he signed up for the royal navy even though he was only sixteen years old.

He sailed the world, but, judging by the stories he brought home, he didn't see much apart from the lowlife taverns he frequented from Port Said to Hong Kong. He managed to survive the First World War and the Dardanelles but was discharged without pension or any recognition for all the years he spent in the king's service. Nonetheless, he was as loyal to the royal family as if he were a royal servant and would get very annoyed with Jerry Slattery, the cobbler, if he didn't celebrate the queen's birthday properly.

'Ventry Calling'

In between Maidhc's house and Bella Browne's lived the dressmaker, Maggie Knightly, and her brother Tom. Nothing in the world bothered Tom but the Kerry football team. He would go on long walks every day and, when he had no other company, he would talk and argue to himself about them. Many's the tongue-lashing he gave to old women for their lack of knowledge about that same team – 'In the name of God, did you ever hear the like of it – Nonny McDonnell and she not knowing who was full forward for Kerry on Sunday'.

The local boyos used to tease him, needless to say. An innocent question was sufficient to send him into orbit. Even though he and Nicholas (Clás) Browne were next door neighbours, an Eskimo and a black man from a sunny clime would understand each other better than those two – one with fluent, rich Irish, the other with lower class, sailors' English even though they were born within an ass' roar of each other.

Poor Bella Browne had nothing in the world but a houseful of cats that she fed far better than herself or Clás. She had pet names on them all – Smokey Blue, Slatey Grey, Ginger, Danny Enright, Cronesberry and the like – and I'd swear they answered to their own names.

Across the road on the sea side of the Colony lived Bill Rooney, his wife Meáig Johnson, and a fine family of daughters as well as a son, Johnnie, from his first marriage. Rooney was also a man who had travelled the world. He fought in the Boer War, he spent a time in the English navy and travelled the United States as a hobo, according to himself, before he settled down in the Colony in

More Neighbours

Ventry and applied himself to rearing his family with discipline and efficiency.

He was a great man in a currach to steady it among submerged rocks. He would be among the first people on the strand in the morning looking for flotsam and jetsam, particularly during the war when anything could come in on the tide – from a coil of rubber to containers of rum. He had wood enough at the back of his house to build a couple of houses. We were all on the lookout for the bounty of the sea and when you hauled your portion above high tide and marked it for yourself, it was in no danger of being stolen.

There was one lad who went to confession to Father Ó Sé and, as a kind of preamble to the sins of the flesh, he confessed that he stole a piece of wreckage. 'I went with a woman,' he continued in a whisper. 'I suppose you did wreckage there too' said the rogue of a priest in such a way that he was heard all over the church!

Rooney was a vigorous, big-hearted man who had his own commonsense philosophy based on his intelligence and his travels. His body was covered in tattoos which he had done in every port where he caroused. He was very proud of the two hounds racing across his belly after a hare who was hurrying for shelter behind his hip.

Nothing went unknown to Rooney, by day or by night, and he watched all the goings on in the neighbourhood with an eagle eye. His wife left her house only to go to mass on Sunday. She took care of Rooney, of her household and of her house in that order and they had all the signs of it. Once when he bought a bicycle, and that was big spending at the time, Tom Néill, the blacksmith who had misgivings about everything and everybody, was looking jealously from the top of the slipway. 'If you saw them above,' he said, 'with the new bicycle, Meáig on one side and Rooney on the other with two cloths and they rubbing it for fear of rust'.

The two brothers Tom and Billy Néill worked in their forge and woe betide anyone who went to Wallace, the other blacksmith in the village. Billy was cantankerous and hostile – a man who spent his youth riding the trains as a hobo in North America. Tom was married to Neilí, a careful housewife, but we were never too sure about which of them she was married to as the three lived in the one house and there was only one bedroom in it – a kind of *ménage à trois* I suppose.

Beside Rooney's was the cobbler's house, Jack Slattery, a widower who lived with his son Jerry and his daughter Joan. Those houses at that side of the Colony were exactly as they had been built almost a hundred years previously for the Soupers, fine, cosy houses, the front door on the sheltered side, a half-door on the sea side of the house outside and a full door inside of it, a strong wooden door that kept out the south-west wind when both doors were shut together. The roof was of tar and felt, the kitchen had an earthen floor and there were two small bedrooms in each house. The windows were very small, placed deep in the thick walls of stone and mud. On stormy days when the back door of the house was tightly shut, the kitchen was warm and comfortable, and on fine days when the door was open there was a fine view of Ventry bay as the sun shone brightly into the kitchen.

The small workshop was in the front corner of the kitchen – a high counter inside the door where Jack and his son worked mending old shoes, heavy, hobnailed shoes for the men and shoes slightly lighter for the women. During the war when there were no new shoes to be bought, the Slatterys spent a period making new shoes from the soles up for the farmers. Jack, with Jerry in tow, would go to the Dingle fair every month to collect the monies due to them – money was scarce and they depended on a good fair, a thing that was not too common in the 1930s. The common cant was 'Put it in the book' or 'I'll see you tomorrow'.

Jack died suddenly one night after he had been chasing a rogue cow of theirs and Jerry came into his inheritance. He immediately set about improving the house – a range in place of the open fire, a back kitchen, a big window overlooking the sea and the shoemaker's shop separate from the kitchen. The poor man had a notion of getting married, of course, but that didn't go down too well with Joan any more than it would with any spinster sister. In the end, Joan gained the upper hand and Jerry spent his life a frustrated bachelor.

It was a delight to visit the shoemaker's shop – the strong smell of leather and the tick-tack-tick of the hammer in rhythm with the shoemaker's rich, venomous, gossip-filled conversation. He spent his time disparaging women who weren't as yet married and he had a sworn hatred of old spinsters; other times he'd be giving out about the priests, and stories and poetry would flow from

'Ventry Calling'

him when he was in full spate. Even though he was an avid reader, he had no recourse to books; nevertheless, anything he ever read he memorised for future use as the opportunity arose.

Jerry Slattery was a strange, pitiful man-without-a-woman who was witty and well-spoken in both Irish and English. May God have mercy on him. Many's the idle hour we passed, killing time in his company, sitting silently on the counter enjoying his non-stop chatter.

Years later when I saw *The Tailor and Ansty* played on stage in the Abbey Theatre by Eamon Kelly and Bríd Ní Loinsigh, I immediately knew the kind of place where Eric Cross had got the basis of his tale. The tailor's shop in Garrynapeaka was of a kind with the shoemaker's shop in Ventry and the pity was that Jerry never read Cross' book. The censorship board made sure of that, along with a couple of arrogant priests.

At the top of the town, next to our house, was Ó Griffín's. Old Mary and her mother were both drawing the old age pension and, when the mother died, her sister Annie came home from America where she had spent forty years working in Yankee houses. Old Mary took to the bed and never again got up out of it.

They were lovely neighbours. Everybody called the returned Yank 'Auntie Annie' or 'The Oul Yank'. Many's the hour I spent in Annie's kitchen smoking cigarettes and listening to the gramophone she brought home from America. 'Victrolla' – an American name – she called it, and it grated a bit on the ears; but, in those pre-radio days, that was a small deficiency. When you'd grow tired of listening to the gramophone, Annie would start on her stories of her life in America and nothing was a match for her but another gramophone. She had a great interest in politics and many times I heard her tell of Al Smith's campaign in 1928, the first Catholic who went for election for the presidency of America. Not unsurprisingly, he failed – the power of the WASPS wasn't yet broken, and, years after the event, she would still weep with sadness at his failure.

She told us how she met Éamon de Valera on the stairs of the Waldorf Astoria in New York in 1919. He was in America collecting money for the Irish Republican cause and she spoke to him in Irish. Long years afterwards when I was guiding Dev around West Kerry on a by-election day in 1957, I told the story to him as we approached Ventry. Annie was out on the road exhorting the voters to vote for Dev and Fianna Fáil when the old Rolls Royce stopped and she recognised who was sitting in front. He told her, without batting an eyelid, that he remembered well the day they met on the stairs of the Waldorf Astoria!

Apart from de Valera, she had only one other hero in her life and that was the pope. She travelled to Rome to see him in the Marian Year, 1954, and she came back a flaming redhead having visited a hairdresser in Paris who swore to her that he could make her beautiful again. From photographs which she kept, you could see that, in her youth, she had been a handsome girl. She had no shortage of admirers, but had no interest in marrying even though she was in love with a fisherman in Dingle whom she loved with all her heart.

'Ventry Calling'

But for Annie, we would have had no knowledge of the olden times when the bay was full of fishing boats from the Isle of Man with their multicoloured sails, dances with the sailors at the crossroads, visits to the gardens in Baile an Ghóilín in the days of Lord Ventry, and stories of the various ministers who lived in the rectory. Her knowledge knew no bounds, nor did her eagerness to share it with anyone who was willing to listen. Her trunks were full of memorabilia from her youth in Ventry and her life in America – hundreds of post cards from every part of the world from Ventry folk who were in the British navy, albums of music from America, dolls, crinoline ladies and a crystal radio set she bought to listen to the results of the Al Smith election in 1928. Little by little, that fine collection got scattered because, as she felt that her end was drawing near, she gave a present to everyone who came her way.

She had good neighbours who took care of her and fed her when she was no longer able to feed herself. She wasn't left on her own. We were fortunate in having her as a neighbour as she was the link between us and the days of her youth and a world that had disappeared.

The last day I saw her was a dark, gloomy winter's day. I was newly married and I brought my young wife, Margery, in to meet her. Although she was eighty-five years old she waltzed around the floor with happiness for us, like a butterfly in a glass jar.

She was dead within a year and we bore her coffin on our shoulders down Poll Gorm to Saint Caitlín's church where she is commemorated in the stained glass window

More Neighbours

behind the altar, a window that is as bright and beautiful as her indomitable, romantic, lively spirit.

A little way outside the village was Mikey Martin's house. Mikey, his wife Kate, and his young family returned from America during the depression and he built a fine stone house, two storeys over the cellar with a dance hall beside it. A new age had arrived, jazz and foxtrots and the luxurious music of the saxophone in the Ballroom of Romance. Dance licences were available at this time even though the clergy weren't too happy with the new dances and the 'jungle music' as they saw it. Now young boys and girls had a place to meet free from sanction and life was bold and reckless. The country was overflowing with young men, no work to be had in the idle 1930s, and their animal instincts were awake on Sunday nights looking for young women.

The roads would be speckled with people going to the dance hall, and then came the war and emigration. Within a few years the country was deserted and the shouts of youth silenced. The 'action' was now in Cricklewood, Camden Town and Hammersmith Broadway. The dance hall was closed, and with it went the dream of freedom and the new life that was promised us with the republic. 'Up Dev' and 'Up the Republic' were fading to a meaningless echo. Mikey Martin, his wife and family went back to America leaving an eerie silence in the place where once there was music and fun and frolicking.

THE FEAST-DAYS OF THE YEAR

When we are young we imagine that time passes by at a snail's pace. It is an eternity from one end of the year to the other, and a lifetime from New Year's Day to Saint Patrick's Day. As we grow older time goes by much more quickly until the years rush by with the speed of a swallow when you reach pension age. No sooner is the holly taken down and the Christmas decorations put safely away than the days begin to grow longer, summer solstice is at the threshold and Christmas is here again.

During Lent, the whole neighbourhood would be in a frenzy as that was the time of year when matches were made in such a way that every man and woman of an age and with the means to get married would be under the Church's yoke by Ash Wednesday. The man would send an 'account' of marriage to the girl he favoured – or to the girl favoured by his family, I should say. One or two of his friends would go with the 'account' taking with them a bottle of whiskey to seal the bargain. There would have been prior knowledge of her dowry and it would be rising the longer she was on the market.

There's many a funny story to be told about those same matches – for instance the one about the young woman who had a lame step. When the man who was set aside for her found out about her defect and was complaining

The Feast-days of the Year

about the trick that had been played on him, the rogue who was responsible retorted: 'In God's name, sure it isn't for racing you want her!'

On another occasion the matchmakers went with an 'account' of matrimony to a young, fair haired girl in Baile Mhic an Daill; the grandfather in the corner, however, sent them home with a different story:

> *Tell you this to Donnchadh an Dúna*
> *Author of all things, tell it true,*
> *That the blind one in the corner*
> *Says this white mare has lost a shoe.*

That was the end of that match!

When Shrove Tuesday came around a wedding would be celebrated in every public house: a barrel of porter on the board, whiskey, wine and biscuits for the women, song, music and the dancing of sets from morning to night.

I remember one day as I was passing through the village of Ballyferriter where a rowdy wedding party was in full sail in Daniel Keane's pub; Father Tom was on duty on the road, an old raincoat he had been given by some garda or other reaching down below his heels to the ground and a safety pin tying it around his neck.

'I suppose,' he said to me, 'that there's high jinks going on at the wedding party'.

You could hear the frolics because we were standing only a few hundred yards from the pub.

'Don't be too hard on them,' I entreated.

'Hard on them, is it?' he retorted. 'Aren't they my own people. If there's no porter or tobacco in heaven, nobody from Ballyferriter will be bothered to go there!'

'Ventry Calling'

The Skellig's Night was the name we gave Shrove Tuesday night. On that night we would go to the houses of the neighbours where man or woman who had yet to wed lived. With an assortment of tin canisters and the like, a dreadful commotion would be raised outside each house in the course of which they would be informed that the boat for the Skelligs was ready, their last chance of marrying before Lent. According to folklore, in ancient times the monks on the Great Skellig hadn't heard of the changes that Pope Gregory had made to the calendar, as a consequence of which Easter was celebrated ten days later there. This custom of ours was not only insulting and intimidating to people who were sensitive about their marital status; it added insult to injury by drawing their attention to it. Worse still was the 'Skellig's List' which would be circulated anonymously, listing the names of these unfortunate people.

The following morning, Ash Wednesday, Lent began – six weeks of fast and abstinence when meat was strictly forbidden every Wednesday and Friday and a person was confined to one main meal and two collations every day but Sunday. We were required to refrain from eating sweets, which was very difficult for us as we lived in a shop.

When Good Friday came around, a dour, dark, hungry day, one was in sight of the promised land and by midday on Easter Saturday Lent was over and how good it felt. On Easter Sunday morning the sun would dance with joy, eggs a-plenty would be boiled for breakfast and the priest would be like a spring lamb dancing on the altar in his bright vestments after the sorrow and solemnity of Lent.

The Feast-days of the Year

After that came May Day when we would put away our shoes and go barefoot, buck-lepping like young calves let out in grass after the long winter. We would go barefoot except on special occasions – Sundays and trips to Dingle – from May Day to the beginning of autumn.

The summer holidays from school were a special delight – long, sunny days as I remember them – days spent swimming and sunning ourselves on the strand or in Poll na Caorach, days spent saving the hay or fishing for wrasse from Pointe na Páirce from where we would go in the currach with Maidhc McDonnell and Bill Rooney, days of new potatoes and fresh vegetables for dinner, of going to bed and rising with the sun, bringing water in barrels to wash ourselves from Bóthar an Uisce. School holidays lasted only five weeks, but they were like an infinity stretching out before us until you'd notice the turning of the days at the end of August as the waning heat of summer heralded the return to school – the smell of chalk and ink and new books.

There were potatoes to be picked after school, lessons to be done by night and the 'long haul' to Hallowe'en. In our house, the children went to the parlour after supper. In the parlour were a large mahogany table, a sofa and a couple of soft seats – furniture my mother bought when Lord Ventry put his great house in Baile an Ghóilín up for auction at the foundation of the Free State. The glass case was full of vessels, glasses and delft from that same house but they were never used, in my youth, except on the day of the station. We all helped each other with our lessons and would all be in bed before nine o'clock. Every-

'Ventry Calling'

body in our house had their own particular task and mine was to prepare a pot of porridge and to leave it beside the range for the morning.

Every night without fail, Seán Nick from Mám an Óraigh would visit our house early, would sit in the same place on the couch and would regale us with stories from far and near. If he happened to be in Dingle of a day, there was no limit to the tidings he would bear and there was no fear that he would spoil a good story for want of invention or imagination in the telling. He was our babysitter, our nursemaid, he was a radio to us, a television when we were growing up and when, suddenly, he stopped visiting our house, much of the pleasure of those winter nights disappeared with him. After thirty years of nightwalking the parting came – and it wasn't Seán was to blame.

After Hallowe'en the darkness descended and it frightened us. Ghost stories and fairy stories like 'The Dog with Eight Legs' and 'The Silent Coach' had a great effect on us. 'The Silent Coach' told of a hearse coming in the night to the house of an innocent person, the horses harnessed to it making no sound. It was an omen of death and shortly afterwards, according to the story, there would be a wake in that house. Needless to say, there was no electric light, only oil lamps that magnified the shadows and the power of the pooka to capture little boys and carry them off to the devil's house. You would go to bed by candlelight, a feather mattress under you, the wind from the west whistling in the slates above you and the sound of the strong sea breaking on the rocks below. In

The Feast-days of the Year

the violence of the storm a shower of lime flakes would fall from the ceiling in such a way that you would imagine the pooka was upon you. There was no cure for it but to cover your head with the sheet and implore your guardian angel to protect you from all evil. My eldest brother, Seán, slept with me and he used not retire until late at night – like the adults. If I awoke in the middle of the night, it was reassuring to feel him outside me in the bed – my guardian angel could attend to his own affairs then – I had a good night and a sound sleep till the morning sun rose again.

A special day in our spiritual calendar was Saint Caitlín's Day, 25 November. We would be let out from school at lunchtime the previous day to go to confession with a warning to be back in class within the hour. Like children everywhere, we would stretch this release from school to as near to dismissal time as we could, and the beating we would receive from the master would be worse than the penance the priest would impose on us in reparation for our sins.

After mass on Saint Caitlín's Day we would visit the graveyard, a custom that stretched right back to Pagan times, like the pattern and the holy wells and the piseogs that were indigenous in the people in spite of the devotions and the catechism. That evening there would be big drinking in the pub, arguments and fights and the singing of songs. To end the evening, when all had drunk their fill, there would be a dance in the hall where would be made, in the words of one of the priests in Dingle, 'the marriage of the cock on the dung heap, the friendship of

'Ventry Calling'

Christ ignored'. From what I've heard, the years have made no alterations in the celebrations of the day, thank God.

The first sign that Christmas was coming was the change in Craig's shop window. It would be decorated with paper chains, masks from Germany – masks such as I saw in Bavaria many years later – tin toys made in Japan, little racing cars that cost but a penny or two, Lucky Bags, also from Japan, and even though they contained only worthless trinkets, you were always expecting the wonders of the world when you opened one.

After much discussion and no little help from Mammy about what presents Father Christmas would bring, it was time to write to Santa Claus. It was also time to be preparing for the Wren and the parcels that had come from England during the year were invaluable to us. There was no chance that Mam would recognise the fine white linen trousers that were worn by the young gentlemen of the navy playing tennis in Dartmouth when they were coloured a vivid green for the Wren.

The post office would be very busy in that final week before Christmas – registered letters from England, dollars from America. Instead of the small handful of letters that usually came, there were now three or four canvas bags full to the brim and there was an extra delivery on Christmas Eve, so much so that my father would have to deliver some letters on Christmas Day itself. There was no overtime or any extra money for this work and he had no choice but to do it.

Of course, you cannot depend on the weather at Christ-

The Feast-days of the Year

mas any more than at any other time of year, but one particular Christmas lingers in my memory. School had been closed for a week, the house had to be cleaned and decorated, the shop was very busy and a large wooden box from Musgrave's in Cork had arrived with our Christmas fare packed in straw – Madeira cakes wrapped in silver paper, tinned fruit, muscatel raisins, sultanas, orange peel, biscuits and other delicacies. A shelf would be full of ling from Newfoundland, there would be a barrel of grapes from Greece, boxes of macaroni from Italy, red apples from France, oranges from Spain – every one of them wrapped in soft white paper.

The weather had cleared, the days were bright and sunny turning to frost come evening. Apart from the heat of summer, no other weather pleased us as much as frosty weather. The colours of the sea and sky would be brilliant at sunset, ice on the road and with the help of a few buckets of water thrown on it at nightfall, we had a fine skating rink. If the icy weather continued, there was the possibility that the pools down by the sandbanks would freeze over and then we'd have sport skating with our hob-nailed shoes. We were being inducted into this by a young lad of the Begleys who had come to live in the village from Quebec and who was a skilled ice-skater. He had brought his skating shoes from Canada and, I can tell you, he gave us an expert and elegant exhibition of ice-skating. He might have been in the Olympics as far as the yokels who had never seen its like were concerned. He was our king as long as the ice lasted and it wasn't long before we were following him out into the deep water with-

'Ventry Calling'

out a care in the world. No other sport could compare with it.

Christmas Eve, a day of fast and abstinence, a day we had for dinner only ling with white sauce, onions and potatoes, the shop and post office a hive of activity, the Christmas candles to be prepared and the crib to be arranged in the window. Then as night fell, out we would go to the height outside our house to view the entire parish. Be certain that a candle would be lighting in every window of Hannafin's at Imleach Slat from three in the evening and then, little by little, every townland would light up – Baile an Chóta, Cill a Ruith, Baile an tSléibhe, Cill Mhic an Domhnaigh all the way back to Cathair an Treantaigh and Cuan, the lovely curve at the foot of Mount Eagle glittering on top of the sea as it would on the night of a full moon.

We would then traverse the village savouring the decorations in every house. You would be enchanted by the silence, the joy, the camaraderie, the peace all around you, and then it was off home for tea – a huge barmbrack and cream loaf with butter and jam and no shortage of any. When the table was cleared after supper, everybody would be given a glass of cordial and then I would try to get to sleep in expectation of Santa.

On Christmas morning, the excitement of the toys laid out on the table and on the couch; going to mass fasting for holy communion, a light covering of snow on top of Mount Eagle and Mount Brandon visible from the church; yeast bread and ham cut from the haunch for breakfast; the long wait for my father to return from delivering the

The Feast-days of the Year

post and then the Christmas dinner around three o'clock in the evening, the darkness falling, the candles lighting – roast turkey, stuffing, mushy peas, sauce and the Christmas pudding that was boiled in a calico bag to finish off the meal.

Saint Stephen's morning, frost on the road from the night before; rising early and dressing up for the Wren – a cloth mask stained with boot polish, the postman's cap; a mouth organ for music, wild gesticulation for dancing, the rat-a-tat-tat of the bodhrán made specially for the occasion.

With regard to the bodhrán, it was a foreign import into Ventry. It so happened that the Curran family spent a year or so in Shanagolden in County Limerick where the father was employed as a teacher of Irish by the Vocational Education Committee. They brought home the skills of the bodhrán people, the manufacture and playing of the bodhrán. All we lacked was a goatskin, something we came upon in Connie O'Brien's coach house. The old sailor, Nicholas Browne, came to our aid with his ingenuity. The goatskin was buried underground until the hairs fell out and then it was seasoned and stretched on a wooden frame. When it was heated by the fireside, the skin would be taut as any drum and there was no limit to the music my friend, Ciarán Curran, would bring from it as he accompanied my mouth organ.

Then around the parish, over ditches, up boreens, only the odd door closed in our faces; a shilling from the schoolmaster, sixpence from special friends and relations, and a load of pennies. Home at nightfall worn and weary; then the counting and dividing of the money, a glass of

'Ventry Calling'

hot claret in our house and a sound sleep.

The following day, an extravagance of spending – bottles of Nash's lemonade from the pub, sweets, fruit and biscuits. On no other day of the year were we so flush with money.

Then the long, dark nights until New Year's Night – The Night of the Great Sharing – when old Annie would pelt a loaf of bread at the back door banishing hunger to the land of the Turks. The year had turned and a cock step would be in every day to Saint Brigid's Day.

In Time of War

I will forever remember that day at the beginning of autumn when the Second World War broke out – 3 September 1939. The long, hot summer of that year was drawing to a close though the heat lingered and the days were sunny. There was a house full of English students in Connie's hotel with a German mistress taking care of them. She cried profusely when she came to the post office to make certain of the news – she had lost her father and brothers in the First World War.

Even though I was only eleven years old, I understood that it was the end of an era and that the world would never be the same again. War was threatening in the two years previous, Hitler and the *Wehrmacht* getting bolder by the day in such a way that they were to be seen on the front page of the *Irish Press* even more than Dev himself. As a consequence, our young lives were growing darker and when war was declared, the shadows descended; the bad times were here again with no prospect of relief until the war ended – six years of depression, of being threatened and even of sadness.

Of course, looking back on it now, the hardship we suffered in Ireland was nothing compared to the devastation, the terror and the killing in England and on the continent but all those years we were anticipating an invasion and bombing of Ireland ourselves.

'Ventry Calling'

Immediately, rationing came in and every man, woman and child got a book of coupons entitling them to a weekly allowance of tea, sugar and butter. The shelves in the shops were bare and many commodities went under the counter – tobacco and cigarettes went scarce before long. No goods from foreign lands were to be seen any more – we didn't see an orange again until the war was over.

In my opinion what most discommoded the people was the scarcity of tobacco. Long years after the war, I met an old man in Cuananna near Caherciveen who used to row his small boat across Dingle bay to Dingle in the hopes of obtaining a half quarter of tobacco. Every shop in the land got its allocation, even though it was small, based on the amount it had purchased before the war. The distribution was fair and well organised under Seán Lemass but that didn't stop the black market which came into being shortly afterwards.

Dishonest shopkeepers left their customers short and sold tea on the black market at £1 per pound weight – big money in 1940. The law was put into effect mercilessly and the black market withdrew deep into the underground.

Butter, flour, clothes and shoes were quickly rationed and there was no petrol available except a very little for those who provided essential services – doctors and the like.

No more coal came from England. Bord na Móna was established to provide the means of supplying heat to the nation and every household cut its own turf. The motto of the government in the 1930s – 'One more sow, one more cow, and one more acre under the plough' – was im-

In Time of War

plemented through compulsory cultivation with inspectors sent to monitor the work. In autumn 1940, there was enough wheat harvested in Ireland to feed the whole country. White, smooth flour was prohibited, and, while the brown wheaten flour we had in its place was a lot more healthy, often it was too moist and heavy to make the best bread though that was but a little fault.

Country folk were better off than city folk from the point of view of feeding because they had plenty of meat and butter, bacon in the barrel and a garden of potatoes and cabbage. All they were missing were the dainties – silk stockings, chocolate, coffee, biscuits, sweets, cakes, jam and white bread and tobacco. There was very little oil for lamps or for making electricity so the country was in the depths of darkness.

There was a shortage of paper: the little that was coming in to the country was made available for the couple of daily newspapers that were published; there was no Sunday newspaper in the country but, little by little, the *News of the World* came in secretly through the post from England and from emigrants but it was strictly forbidden by the priests.

There was a strong censorship of the affairs of the day: this was to prevent the enemy from obtaining information about the country. When Germany learned that we were busily preparing to resist any attack that would be made on our country, Lord Haw Haw, in his programme *Germany Calling*, informed us that we were in no such danger, that we could sleep safely in our beds at night as Germany was more interested in oil wells than in holy

'Ventry Calling'

wells! The few radios that were in the village depended on wet batteries that were quickly exhausted. They were turned on only for the news, but there was great demand for Haw Haw's programme. He was a fluent speaker, concise and very knowledgeable about the daily affairs of Ireland and England. He mocked the things the English held most dear – 'their stuttering king and their bandy-legged queen' to quote but one example. They didn't forgive him. When the war was over, William Joyce (Lord Haw Haw), of Irish stock although born in New York, was sentenced to death and hanged in the Tower of London under a Norman act dating from the twelfth century. There was no end to their desire to exact revenge on the Irishman who mocked them during the war.

The name of every place, post office and school was obliterated and all the road signs were taken down so that the invader would be confused when the attack came.

All the young men and women had gone to England in search of work and money – two things that weren't available at home. When they became accustomed to the freedom of England, most of them never again returned except, maybe, on holiday. You could almost say, like the time of the Elizabethan wars in Ireland in the sixteenth century, that there wasn't the lowing of a cow or a baby's cry to be heard from Dunquin to Cashel.

Many of the young men joined the army and, although Haw Haw said of the Irish army that they could not chase the tinkers from Puck Fair, we would have been a lot worse off without them. The Local Defence Force was established – a kind of *Dad's Army* shabbily dressed,

In Time of War

.303 rifles and five bullets apiece to keep the forces of the king of the world out of Ventry harbour.

The Irish transport system was a shambles, a few buses with a few trains running on wet turf and nobody knew when they would arrive at their destination. There was no rubber available and even the bicycles were hung up for want of tyres.

During all that time there was, among those left at home, a wave of patriotism sweeping the country, loyalty to the nation uppermost with an accompanying anti-English feeling, even though Ireland depended entirely on England for the necessities of life. The English were not too unhappy with that, as England was depending on our meat, butter and food to feed its population.

There is no doubt that a large majority of Irish people were in favour of Germany. The memory of the Black and Tans was still fresh – England's grip on Ireland had been relaxed only eighteen years previously and the Union Jack was flying over the ports of Berehaven, Cobh and Lough Swilly until 1938. We would have been happy to see the Germans laying into our old enemy even though many of our people depended on the registered letters from England to sustain them. Most of the Irish who emigrated had no secondary education and the clergy and the wealthy classes held them in low esteem.

When they went to England, they found employment, they had money in their pockets and they were fairly treated. They gave their allegiance to England and turned their backs on an Ireland of unemployment, an Ireland that was uncharitable and narrow minded. The women came home on holiday with English men and at mass on Sundays it was obvious that those same men had no experience of how to deport themselves in church – signing themselves with the cross or genuflecting when the women did, the old women in the village backbiting and deriding them.

They adopted an English tone – 'Have you been ofa, have you seen Charlie?' One day a girl came into the shop to purchase a couple of loaves of bread for the *meitheal* – 'whatever that may be', she said, denying her native tongue that she now felt would restrict her in her new life. On the other hand, one of the Englishmen asked my father for a 'piper' one day – the Cockney wanted a newspaper – and my father went off in search of a pipe for him!

Both cultures were competing with each other once again. In the dance hall, jazz was in fashion, the slow foxtrot and the palais glide, and the idiots at home in a tangle attempting to master these new steps. The priests were in a frenzy going on about these 'alien influences' that were arriving from 'Pagan England', and the young women were beginning to drink glasses of beer in the pubs as they saw their counterparts doing in England. In their Sunday sermons, the priests would rail against the 'jungle music', the 'cocktails' and the assault being made on holy Ireland by the agents of the devil. There was mention of contraceptives, but nobody dared use them, or if they did, they kept it to themselves. As Peaitnín said in confession when the priest was trying to find out what woman he was servicing: 'I know what's on your mind, my boyo, but don't think you'll find out what's in mine!'

In Time of War

In the beginning, the war was waged mostly at sea, a fight to the death between the U-boats and the convoys, large ships laden with munitions sailing from America which were being sent to the bottom by the U-boats. The U-boats were successful until radar was introduced and from then on the tide turned in favour of the vessels sailing on, not below, the sea.

Fishermen in Dingle would find the skeletons of sailors caught in their nets and, once, they came ashore with a lifeboat full of corpses. On the tide would come flotsam from the boats that were sunk out at sea and, every now and then, explosives which the army would decommission.

One foggy evening in the month of October, the war came home to us in a very special way when, at about four o'clock a U-boat sailed into Dúinín at the mouth of the bay. The story spread like wildfire after my father had informed the superintendent of the garda síochána in Dingle and we all scurried to Rinn Stiabhna, a mile back the road from home. The submarine was anchored only twenty yards from the rocks and the crew of a Greek ship, the *Diamantes*, were being put ashore, four at a time, in a rubber dinghy. The *U35* had sunk the *Diamantes* with three torpedoes after they had taken the crew, twenty-eight sailors in all, on board.

As this was still the beginning of the war, there was a kind of chivalric custom among sea captains to spare the lives of the crews and to put them ashore at the nearest land. That is how the *U35* sailed easily into Ventry harbour and put the Greek crew ashore in full view of the whole countryside. The entire operation took just about an hour and, before the garda síochána arrived on the scene, the *U35* had sailed out a couple of hundred yards from the coast and had submerged beneath the waves. The Greeks were taken to Dingle hospital and we gathered empty cigarette boxes and chocolate wrappers that the Germans had left behind them as souvenirs of the occasion.

Before the captain bade farewell to the Greek sailors, the story went around that he had informed them that Michael Long would take care of them. Michael Long had a public house at the pier head in Dingle where Máire de Barra's pub was later on, and he operated as an agent for Lloyd's. The German captain had been on holiday in Dingle before the war and had got to know Michael Long. As he said goodbye to the Greeks, he told them to have a pint there and to remember him to Michael Long.

That was at the beginning of the war. With the passage of time, the war at sea deteriorated, and all that came ashore were corpses and skeletons picked clean by the seagulls. That valiant captain who sailed his submarine to within a man's jump of that wild coast returned to Ireland a couple of years ago and revisited the scene of that landing. He drank a pint or two in Michael Long's pub and visited the hospital where there is a plaque to the memory of those Greek sailors he saved from the sea all those years ago.

When Germany invaded Russia unexpectedly in June 1941, it was like a release from the gallows for us in Ireland. We were no longer under threat as the war was now directed to the east, places far overseas – Leningrad, Stalingrad, the Don and even Moscow itself. We were well pleased that those two giants were fighting to the death on the frozen steppes of Russia.

From then on, Germany was subjugated, day-by-day the allies were gaining the upper hand and the war at sea was as good as over. The *Flying Fortresses* began to fly from America in preparation for D-Day. Sometimes the sky would be full of them in squadrons to the horizon and it was an awesome sight. Then one day in the summer of 1944 Domhnall Ó Cíobháin came into the classroom in Coláiste Íosagáin in Ballyvourney where I was a student and told us the amazing story of the invasion of the continent every bit as well as the BBC.

Within the year, the war was over, Germany was crushed and rent, and the dark clouds of those six years of war were dispersing all over the world. The first sign we got within a week that peace was with us again was that oranges were on sale in Ua Luasa's shop in Ballyvourney and that evening we had white bread, as much of it as we could eat, on the table at teatime. The days of our youth were running out, and though we didn't know it yet, the old life, the old ways were disappearing forever.

The Golden Age

The rain was falling in torrents on the cement square, the evening was dark and bleak, nothing to be seen through the window but bare gable-ends and fir trees like ghosts behind them. It was the beginning of autumn 1942 and a group of us had just arrived in a hackney car from Dingle to Coláiste Íosagáin in Ballyvourney to begin six years of training in the craft of teaching.

Even though I had been looking forward to it for a couple of months, the loneliness and homesickness were erupting in me in this strange place where nobody knew anybody else. After supper we went to the dormitory where everybody had his own cubicle and we prepared to go to sleep. This was the first time most of us were wearing pyjamas and one young boy from West Cork who was just across the passage from me was observing me intently to see what I would do as he hadn't a clue what to do himself. There was a sink with hot and cold water in each cubicle, a small white press above it for toothpaste and Brylcream and another press for our clothes, a fine, comfortable iron bed with white starched sheets and linoleum on the floor sparkling with polish under our feet. It was like being in a posh hotel.

The following morning I woke with a start to the noise

The Golden Age

of a bell ringing through the dormitory and the sonorous voice of Brother Anastás announcing the day. The sun was shining, the rain had cleared and the fragrant smell of the fir trees wafted in through the window. Down we went to mass followed by a fine breakfast in the refectory and then out into the beautiful morning for our first sight of the playing fields, the gables, the brilliant Sullane river and the surrounding woods. Bliss was it to be alive.

Coláiste Íosagáin was established as a Preparatory College for trainee national teachers by the De la Salle Brothers in 1939. In the mid 1930s the government decided to build a new school in the Muskerry Gaeltacht for that purpose. Forty-one acres were bought in Ballyvourney and the building commenced.

It was a beautiful location – a fertile plain in the Sullane river-basin, the Derrynasaggart mountains a defensive wall to the north, the road to Cork winding eastwards through Poll na Bró and escaping through the Ballyhoura Mountains to Killarney. Sliabh Daimh and the Paps guarded the old gods to the north along with Cathair Chraobh Dhearg. On one side of it was a sheltered, leafy wood on the mountainside leading to Saint Gobnait's graveyard where the poet Seán Ó Ríordáin, and Seán Ó Riada are now taking their rest. There was a mystery, a magic and a sense of history about this place that had a special effect on every scholar that came under its influence.

When the building was ready, there was room for more than 200 scholars; six spacious dormitories and every boy had his own cubicle. All the floors were covered with the same heavy linoleum that was on the floors of the *Queen*

Ventry One

Mary and the college had its own generator to provide it with electricity. In the refectory were tables and heavy oak forms that came from the Royal Hospital in Kilmainham as a present from the Board of Works. There were three football fields laid out along with tennis courts, ball alleys, spacious lawns and a sunken lake with water plants and fish in front of the main door. Without a doubt in the world, Coláiste Íosagáin was the flagship of educational establishments when the first class crossed the threshold.

Who were these students that were so well treated by the new state? Entrance examinations to these Preparatory Colleges were held at Easter week every year. These examinations were for young scholars between the ages of thirteen and fifteen years and were run by the Department of Education. About twenty-five would get 'the call' on the strength of this examination and there were a certain number of places reserved specifically for students from the Gaeltacht. Nobody was denied education for want of means; it was free for those whose families could not afford to pay, and, in addition, there was a clothes allowance, a travel allowance and even a generous allowance of pocket money, too.

These Preparatory Colleges had a strong social philosophy that was very progressive compared to the rather narrow secondary system of education that was available at the time. The system was based on Pearse's ideal in Coláiste Éanna – education through the medium of Irish provided in an independent and liberal atmosphere. There was no corporal punishment, for example, and the boys had permission to smoke tobacco – two things that were

The Golden Age

unusual, to say the least, at that time. The aim was to bring students of the first quality from the various *Gaeltachtaí*, to mingle them with gifted students from the non Irish speaking parts of Ireland up to Leaving Certificate level, and then train them as national teachers in Saint Patrick's College, Drumcondra, so that there would be expert and fluent teachers available to revive the Irish language throughout the country. There was a wide curriculum; Latin and Greek were included for those who required them. There was a magnificent laboratory in which were taught physics, chemistry and biology. Woodwork, drawing and art were taught to train the hand and the eye. Traditional and classical music were taught. The students learned Irish dance and there was a great emphasis on debating, drama and choral singing. It is obvious that the syllabus was in keeping with the fine, modern building, and, by comparison with contemporary schools, the comprehensive system of the Preparatory Colleges was fifty years ahead of its time. 'The golden age', Brother Peadar christened this period in our education. The students were clever enough to gain honours in the Leaving Certificate examination by themselves so that the teachers could do what they pleased, or, in some cases, nothing if it so pleased them.

There were talented teachers on the staff – two versatile Kerrymen among them, Domhnall Ó Cíobháin from Gorta Dubha and Brother Peadar Ó Loingsigh from Valentia island. Domhnall was one of the most fluent, accomplished Gaelic speakers we ever heard. When he recited one of the lays of the Fianna, a magical hush would

'Ventry Calling'

fall on the class and his voice would be like the murmur of the Sullane on a May morning:

> *Ag seilg dúinn maidin cheoigh*
> *In imeallbhordaibh Locha Léin*
> *Mar a raibh crainn ba chumhra bláth*
> *Is ceol gach tráth go binn ag éin.*

Or again:

> *Ceol lena gcoladh Fionn go moch*
> *Lachain ó Log na dTrí gCaol,*
> *Scaltarnach luin Doire an Chairn,*
> *Is búithreadh an daimh ó Ghleann na gCaor.*
> *Fead an Fhiolair ó Ghleann na mBua*
> *Nó ó scairt chruaidh Dhruim le Sruth*
> *Cearca fraoigh é Chruchain Chuinn*
> *Nó fead dobhráin ó Dhruim dá Chon.*

It was as good as a night at the opera. Domhnall taught us history too, and he was so enthusiastic about the French Revolution that one year he forgot that the French Revolution was not on the syllabus. He loved to tell of 'the long necked women of Paris knitting at the foot of the guillotine' and of Louis XIV – 'he was weak, he was lazy, he was lascivious' and we were so enthralled with his telling that we didn't care if it was on the syllabus or not. When Domhnall found out his mistake, three weeks before the Leaving Certificate, a feverish crash-course began in an attempt to cover the course. He gave us an account of Napoleon's assault on Russia in a couple of terse words: 'advanced, was defeated, retreated'. I wonder to whom can we attribute the fact that many of us got honours in history that year!

The Golden Age

Concerning Brother Peadar, his knowledge of the history and folklore of Muskerry and Duhallow was unsurpassed and he had a greater interest in them than he had in the English language – 'the language of the English', as he was wont to call it, although he was nominally our English teacher. He had a master's degree in English from Cambridge. He generously shared his knowledge of the locality with us, and there was no place, east or west, within a day's journey that he didn't bring us on our days off. We became expert on the countryside from Carriganimmy to Beaufort and Lios Carragáin, and from Coolea to Réidh na nDoirí.

Often when the day would be fine Brother Seosamh would call a holiday out of the blue with the excuse that it was the birthday of some obscure saint from Italy or Spain. Sometimes the day would be given over to 'national work' as he termed it. We were in the middle of the war, of course, and this kind of work was very fashionable. According to the season, we would spend those days setting trees and sowing plants and becoming acquainted with nature unknown to ourselves. One year, we made a swimming pool in the river and when the fine summer days arrived we spent all our spare time swimming and diving like seals, or lying, belly to sun, on the riverbank. When the floods of winter came it was swept away but its remains are to be seen yet as an example of the social vision, without grants or Fás schemes, that was fostered in those times. *'Eine stunde für das Vaterland'*, the Germans termed this kind of work which helped them build up their country from the rubble after the war.

The Spiddal Kid's Adventure

It began when the president's, Brother Seosamh, father died. We always imagined that that same brother had not been conceived so much as moulded from some foreign material.

He was a stout, vigorous man who had energy above the ordinary as was obvious to us when there was 'national work', as he called it, to be done. He had a head of thick, grey hair, cut like Saint John Bosco – a kind of crew cut that wasn't too bare in such a way that you'd think it was a wig as nobody had ever seen the sign of a barber's hand on it. In the same way, we never saw him wearing a suit of clothes, but a soutane with the rectangular collar split in the middle that was worn by the De la Salle Brothers.

He was hot tempered and hostile, and, although he was a classical scholar, he had no understanding of teenagers as far as we could see. There was no friendship between him and the boys and the only time you would be in his company would be when you had to explain some misdemeanour or other. Because he had the power to expel students from the college, and the name of not being unwilling to do so, we stayed out of his way as far as we could. Sometimes when he came to the refectory to supervise supper he would be calm, even sleepy, which made us suspect that he was hitting the bottle again –

The Spiddal Kid's Adventure

particularly when he would be chewing the cud to hide the smell of the alcohol.

The story spread throughout the college – 'Josie's' father was dead and he would be away from college for a week. It was like a licence to do what we wished as, in truth, the only one we paid any heed to was 'Josie'. That night after supper, when we had an hour to spend in the recreation room, a group of the senior students planned to go down the village without permission.

It was a moonlight night at the end of autumn, a touch of frost in the air and the full moon rising over Saint Gobnait's graveyard up above. We were full of ardour and bravado in search of any adventure that would befall us, half drunk on the fresh night air and the freedom – full of the desire and folly of youth. We roamed wildly through the countryside but every door was closed and nobody else was out under the sky but ourselves. It was enough for us that we were free under the light of the moon with no fetters on us for an hour. We were quiet as mice again for late study, the rosary and bed. These high jinks lasted the whole week.

There were three boys, however, for whom this was not sufficient and, with their blood up in the mystery of the night, they began to seek other ways of satisfying their desires. The servant girls who attended to the tables and did the housework had private rooms behind the college with private stairs leading to them and they were strictly out of bounds. It wasn't long before the young stallions braved the porches and made their way up to the girls with whom they had made dates during the day on the understanding that their doors would not be locked.

When Brother Seosamh returned, that put an end to our forays into the village, but now the three boys had beaten a path to the private stairs. Things continued so until one night, one of the girls wouldn't admit her lover. Up with my boyo to the parlour looking for other delicacies and he took a couple of deep swigs from the whiskey bottle. He left through the window and proceeded to a level roof outside his beloved's bedroom. He lit a cigarette while he pondered how to persuade her to let him in.

Professor Ó Flannagáin was returning to his room at the back of the building when he saw the lighted cigarette at the window. He became suspicious and woke Brother Seosamh. It wasn't long until the Spiddal Kid was captured with the information that two more of his companions were in their ladies' quarters. The brothers, too, were forbidden to go into the 'harem' and Brother Raphael was posted on guard at the bottom of the stairs while the Spiddal Kid was being interrogated in the office. Cadbury, the second student, came down and was immediately apprehended but there was a long wait for the third party. Raphael grew tired and went in search of a chair. In the few moments when the brother was not at his station, the third culprit came down the stairs and returned to his bed where he slept soundly till morning blissfully unaware of the drama that was taking place all around him.

The Spiddal Kid and Cadbury were sent home on the bus the following morning and then began the investigation. Who was the one that got away? The Department of Education was informed without delay and a heavy gang

The Spiddal Kid's Adventure

from that same department descended upon us under the chief inspector who was christened 'Ears of the Well'. This was before Clouseau's time!

We were all interrogated about the affair and the third culprit's surname was obtained from one of the servant girls but that was the only piece of information they divulged. They were safe enough in that as there were five boys of that surname in the college and they were all happy to deny that they had anything to do with the affair. The authorities failed to proceed any further with the investigation; nobody informed on the lover boy although the whole college knew who he was. The inspectors returned to Dublin but Brother Seosamh, who was now being blamed for neglect of duty, continued with the investigations. It was usual for boys to be awakened from their sleep in the middle of the night and questioned, but all to no avail. We went home for the Christmas holidays badly shaken but with the information still deeply hidden.

During the holidays, Brother Seosamh visited the orphanage in Cork city to intimidate a harmless, gentle boy who had succeeded in obtaining a place in Coláiste Íosagáin. The brother accused him of being up the stairs on that fateful night. The poor boy had no one in this world to defend him and he broke easily. Immediately the third culprit was informed that he need not return to the college.

The rest of us returned subdued to the college after the Christmas holidays. It wasn't long before the incident in the orphanage became known and then began the ugly, cowardly campaign against poor McCarthy. He was boycotted mercilessly, he was singled out as a spy, the poor orphan was pursued in such a way that he had no peace, day or night, and, as is usual in these cases, those with the least grievance were the hardest against him.

We finished our course in Ballyvourney under a cloud and graduated to Saint Patrick's College that autumn. McCarthy was still in Ballyvourney and he came into the training college the following year. 'The third man' sat his leaving certificate in his own school at home and succeeded in obtaining a place by open competition in the training college because the civil servants failed to recognise him as the person who was expelled from Coláiste Íosagáin.

After a couple of weeks, by accident, Father Ó Tuama, the president of the college, discovered the mistake and he hurried to the Minister of Education, Dick Mulcahy, to inform him of the problem. Father Ó Tuama advised him not to interfere with the *status quo*, but the military man, General Mulcahy, was adamant that things be put right.

A post in the civil service was created for 'the third man' and poor McCarthy was advised to leave the college and go overseas. I never heard of him again. The Spiddal Kid was killed on service with the RAF; Cadbury, the star-struck boy who was so smitten with his first love, died shortly afterwards without reaching his twentieth year; Brother Seosamh was relieved of his post in Coláiste Íosagáin and was banished to Mauritius as librarian where he died a few years later. Those of us who were on the periphery of these tragic events will never forget the treachery

The Spiddal Kid's Adventure

that was perpetrated on that gentle, lonely orphan. Never.

Looking back on these events with the perspective of the years and in the context of today, what was all the commotion about? They were young, spirited men doing no harm to anybody and they were only following their natural instincts. When I see the teenagers of today, boys and girls comfortable in each other's company, with a fine healthy attitude to sex, I think how well it is for them.

In Ireland of the 1940s and for a long time afterwards, Big Brother was watching you constantly, lust was a mortal sin that would damn you to the depths of hell and life was hard and inhospitable to orphans.

Saint Patrick's College and Dublin

The war was over for a year but, nonetheless, life was getting worse. The world economy was so much out of kilter that it took a number of years for the big wheels of that economy to function again. Oil was still unavailable and there wasn't even one lump of coal to operate the trains. They were depending on turf to power their steam engines which proved a poor substitute.

In 1946 the weather was so wet that the turf couldn't be harvested and the government had to send out the army to the bogs and meadows to save the turf and hay. Large tracts of the Phoenix Park were under wheat, barley and potatoes, and ricks of turf that stretched as far as the eye could see were brought in from the bogs in the centre of Ireland but the turf was soft and wet. Useless turf! In the year of 1946 we turned our faces towards Dublin for the first time, having been looking forward to it for six years.

It was a hazardous, boring journey. We left Ventry, my friend Jack and I, at four o'clock in the morning to catch the bus to Tralee, and when we arrived at Tralee railway station we were informed that the train to Dublin had been cancelled for want of turf. We were put on a bus to Limerick, which we reached at about one o'clock in the afternoon, to catch the Dublin train which was scheduled

Saint Patrick's College and Dublin

to depart at three o'clock. Alas! It was almost midnight before the train pulled out and we were without heat, without food or drink except for the dry sandwich we had the good sense to bring with us from a pub near the station. From that till morning, the train was stopping and starting trying to build up a head of steam until, at long last, we arrived at our destination, Kingsbridge Station – Heuston Station now – at eight o'clock in the morning.

There were no buses running, only trams – and they weren't operating at that hour, so six of us got a ride in a horse drawn carriage. That was how we reached Saint Patrick's Teachers' Training College in Drumcondra and, even though we were worn and weary from the journey from the dawn of the previous day, it was wonderful to be in Dublin. The city was clear and bright in the morning sun. The River Liffey was like a huge road with the Guinness steam barges carrying their cargo of barrels, busily travelling between the brewery and the port. When they reached O'Connell Bridge at high tide, they had to take off the chimney and lay it on the deck in case it wouldn't pass under the bridge where the Gardiner Street rabble would incite them with 'Bring us back a canary!' We, the country boys, were in the carriage with our mouths open.

We went up O'Connell Street, the General Post Office on our left, all the while imagining Pearse reading the Proclamation of the Irish Republic in front of it, the proclamation that began all the commotion in this country, a commotion that is with us yet. We registered in the college, ate a hearty breakfast and went off down the city again to see the other wonders it had to offer.

'Ventry Calling'

The city was still depending on trams for transport and, as a transport system, it was not to be faulted. However, people like Todd Andrews weren't satisfied until an end was put to that fine means of transport which resulted in the city being choked with traffic today. No other city in Europe is as badly served for public transport as Dublin. Like a lot of things the English left us as an inheritance, we were only too willing to get rid of them without heeding the old adage – 'one look before you is worth two looks behind'.

We had to spend two years in Saint Patrick's in order to become qualified as national teachers and, despite the shortages, the cold, the hunger and lack of money, we enjoyed our time there. The college president was Father Diarmuid Ó Tuama, an educationalist and gentleman of the highest order. He was originally from Castleisland and he belonged to the Vincentian order. He treated the students well. His motto was that we were now young men until we proved otherwise, and the one rule he put before us was to leave our girlfriends outside the college gates. Such freedom! We were at the threshold of life in the charge of a man who understood and respected us.

But his modern ideas of personal freedom and such weren't in agreement with the ideas of the archbishop, John Charles McQuaid, who lived in a grand palace nearby. The archbishop was a man of sour disposition, arrogant and severe who was called, behind his back, 'The Druid of Drumcondra', and woe betide anyone who crossed him.

Within two years, Father Ó Tuama was banished to London in charge of Strawberry Hill, a Catholic teachers'

Saint Patrick's College and Dublin

training college, a place, the archbishop considered, where he could do no harm. When McQuaid returned from Rome later on, having spent a year arguing over the changes in the Church as part of the Second Vatican Council, he reminded the faithful that there would be no changes 'that would disturb their simple faith'.

The churches were full to overflowing with people. The poor of the city with ten and more in family were living in single rooms in tenements in Gardiner Street, in Mountjoy Square and Corporation Place. According to McQuaid, a dreadful curse would fall on the country if contraceptives were used to control the numbers of children in families the likes of which wouldn't be seen outside of Calcutta. We used visit them every week under the auspices of the Society of Saint Vincent de Paul to bring them what aid we could, and they were in a sorry state.

The bordellos of 'Monto', that is Montgomery Street, were closed down by the Legion of Mary and the prostitutes were plying their trade on the streets; they were dirty, unkempt and vulgar. There was an old prostitute we called 'Woodbine Annie' on the pavement at the bottom of Dorset Street. She was shrunken with age and disease, having spent a wretched lifetime trying to fend for her large family. When Doctor Noel Browne attempted to relieve the suffering of those people with his Mother and Child Scheme, the archbishop, in collusion with the Irish Medical Association, ensured his removal from government. They were of the opinion that control of the poor should be left exclusively in the hands of the hierarchy and wealthy doctors.

'Ventry Calling'

The city was full of mean pubs, the smell of porter and tobacco coming out the door from the darkness within, and half hungry, drunken men staggering around the streets. Porter was cheap and it was stronger than it is now: it cost five pence for a pint of 'plain' and seven pence for a pint of 'Double X'.

No self-respecting woman would be seen near a pub, but there were snugs for the prostitutes in many establishments. There was one such snug in Lloyd's pub in North Earl Street and it was called 'the Chamber of Horrors'. Of course, upper class women used to patronise the lounge bars in the Gresham, the Metropole, the Russell and other posh hotels, and they could drink all they liked in comfort with the few who practised that lifestyle.

There was hardly any beer available in the pubs, but one pub at the bottom of Gardiner Street (Doran's lounge bar) had cold, frothy lager from Munich in barrels. I have never tasted beer like it. Though Dublin was a drunken, rakish city in those days, all the pubs closed at closing time.

The pubs closed for an hour in the middle of the day. 'The Holy Hour' it was called and the reason for it was that the boozers would go home and their pattern of drinking would be broken. When the pubs closed at half past ten at night, there was great demand for horse drawn carriages to transport the drunks three miles from the city centre to places like The Goat in Goatstown and The Dead Man in Lucan where they would be considered *bona fide* travellers and thus entitled to be served drink until midnight.

Saint Patrick's College and Dublin

There were places like Dolly Fawcett's in Capel Street that had a bad reputation, and where you could drink illegal beverages, poitín or 'Red Biddy', after-hours. It was frequented by off duty prostitutes, students out on the town, and detectives from Dublin Castle looking for information, and the law left her alone because the establishment was like a monitoring station for the civic guards. There were clubs, like the Teachers' Club in Parnell Square, which operated under a different law and where you could drink till morning without interference.

If they still hadn't enough to drink, there were people mad enough to visit the markets which opened at six o'clock in the morning to cater for the market people and farmers who used to drive their beasts to the big fairs. These were the out-and-out dipsos who used go to the dog show in Ballsbridge looking for drink on Saint Patrick's Day, a day when all the pubs were closed in the city. Once as Brendan Behan was coming out of the toilet there, he was knocked down when he fell over a poodle on a lead. He turned on the lady who owned the poodle with: 'What a fucking place to bring a dog!'

Up in Saint Stephen's Green the Georgian houses had underground cellars called 'the Catacombs' and there was no end to the antics that went on there if we can believe J. P. Donleavy in his book *The Gingerman*. Needless to say, we, country boys, had no recourse to these places but, as the saying goes, if we didn't go to 'school' ourselves, we met the scholars coming home!

On Sunday nights we used go to the céilí that was run by Ailtírí na hAiséirí in Harcourt Street – an out of tune

'Ventry Calling'

piano, fiddles and drums, the sweat pouring from the musicians and dancers during the Siege of Ennis, the Walls of Limerick and the Fairy Reel, a scarcity of women and a surfeit of men as admission was free to the boys of Saint Patrick's.

Then, on Wednesday nights, you would get in to the dance at the Teachers' Club for half price – 'skivvies' night out' it was called – but if you had the entrance fee to the National Ballroom or the Four Provinces or the Crystal you might chance to meet the young, vigorous nurses from the Rotunda or the Mater – 'Do you come here often? ... The night is hot ... Maybe you'd like to walk out in the air?' The most popular pastime in Dublin in those years was, of course, the cinema. There would be long queues stretching up and down O'Connell Street from midday waiting for the cinemas to open, a bag of sweets and a 'package of fags' to take in with you, carpets and soft seats, heat and comfort from inclement weather and farfetched films – Alan Ladd and Bing Crosby, John Wayne and other killers of a hundred, and starlets like Ava Gardner, Rita Hayworth and Deanna Durbin.

In the Capitol and the Theatre Royal there would be an hour-long stage show before the film. It would begin with the Royalettes or the Rockettes, beautifully choreographed, dancing on the stage, followed by a comedy act, a magic act, 'One Fine Day' sung by the baritone Seán Mooney or 'Dublin on a Sunny Sunday Morning' from Noel Purcell. Big stars like Danny Kaye, Paul Robeson, Nat King Cole and Red Skelton came regularly to perform in the Theatre Royal.

Saint Patrick's College and Dublin

Even though the Hollywood films were insipid and silly, people thought it was the high point of sophistication to have seen them. Liam Mac Gabhann used to review them in the *Irish Press* on Mondays and his reviews were far superior to the films he sent up. There was no decline in cinema audiences, however, until the television age. The Theatre Royal and the Regal beside it were knocked to make way for government offices. The Capitol was closed and the Rockettes dispersed, those girls we once thought so attractive under the footlights. The day came when the Metropole in O'Connell Street closed and that was of the same magnitude as the blowing up of Nelson's Pillar.

When we entered the training college in 1946, the teachers' strike was under full sail. A young teacher's salary starting out was £2.14s. per week for working in freezing and dirty classrooms. The teachers were in dire straits. They were all of country stock; nobody from Dublin would put themselves forward to become teachers and, for that reason, all the teachers were emigrants to the city. There was no way out for them as many were married with mortgages, but on the other hand, many had fallen under the spell of the city and had no desire to return to the country again.

During the summer, young teachers used go to Britain to earn extra money to buy a winter coat or a bicycle, or to clear their debts for another year. They would perform every kind of slavery there from the hydro-electric dams in Scotland to the sweatshops in London – Lyon's Corner House, night work in the creameries or work with 'Mac-

'Ventry Calling'

Alpine's Fusiliers'. I myself spent one pleasant summer picking strawberries in Norfolk. You would have a few days of enjoyment in London before you returned to your classroom to teach without a break until Christmas. It's no wonder they went on strike – they had no other choice.

They were left out on strike for seven months and they had to return to work without any satisfaction. In September of that year, Kerry and Roscommon were playing in the All Ireland football final and, in consequence, there were large crowds in the city. The teachers paraded through the city centre on the Saturday evening, and on the following day they were at the head of the crowds attempting to enter Croke Park for the match so that they would have the principal place on the sideline.

At half time, suddenly, there were 500 teachers in the middle of the park with their flags and posters and the demonstration began in a peaceful and orderly manner. Dev and Seán T. O'Kelly, the president of Ireland, were in the Hogan Stand and they were none too pleased with what they saw. It wasn't long before a strong force of the garda síochána came on the scene and they scattered the teachers in all directions. One man escaped the melee, however, and he continued to run around the field with his poster with the police in hot pursuit. Of course Séamus Ó Dubhda from Muiríoch wasn't without the use of his legs when he was picked to play at midfield for Dublin a couple of years previously, and he left the policemen floundering in his wake.

The result of all this was that a new political party, Clann na Poblachta, was founded by Seán MacBride and many teachers joined it. Within two years the Fianna Fáil government fell, having been in office for sixteen consecutive years. Teachers got a raise in pay, their working conditions were reviewed, and their traditional allegiance to Fianna Fáil was broken forever. 'Far back into the distance stretch the relics of a bad deed'.

Over in Drumcondra under the suspicious eye of Archbishop McQuaid, our two years passed by in grand style. My brother Seán, who was an army officer by this time, was stationed in the Curragh, and Maidhc was in the air force in Baldonnell. My two brothers shared generously with me so that the poverty of the student's life didn't impinge too much on me. They both died young before I could repay their kindness.

Every Sunday morning a couple of army lorries would arrive to transport us to Portobello Barracks where we would spend the morning under arms and in uniform on the barracks square with 'Right, Left, Right!', 'Eyes Right!', 'Present arms!', 'Lower arms'. We were in the Pearse regiment of the Local Defence Force and, if it did nothing else for us, it put the appearance of soldiers on us, and we had fine brown shoes to knock sparks off the streets of Dublin that harsh, inclement winter of 1946–47. After lunch there would always be a game in Croke Park or a soft seat in the Carlton or the Savoy if the weather was too bad to go to Croke Park.

We were reasonably well trained to teach with skill and authority, though I must admit that we learned more from our fellow teachers throughout the city. During the year, we would be sent out to the schools for two three-

'Ventry Calling'

week periods of teaching practice. Having spent your term in Rutland Street or City Quay, you were fit to teach any class, anywhere. Both those schools catered for the families of dockers – tough men who could take a large portion of Guinness' daily output on board. The schools were much like the area in which they were situated, full of rats and filth and hopelessness. The revolution didn't do much for these followers of James Connolly – they were still, and for many years afterwards, in the slough of despond.

When, later on, I began my teaching career in Cabra West, things were much the same. Cabra West was a new suburb on the outskirts of Dublin. It had a fine new school of two storeys with a beautiful view of the Dublin mountains. 'Twenty men from Dublin town/Drilling on the mountainside' was the anthem of the old city stock now in exile in the countryside, as they saw it.

They were moved from the heights on the banks of the Liffey where they had been living since the time of the Vikings. They had no knowledge of rural life or culture. They thought milk came from a bottle and when the huge herds of cattle came down the Navan Road to the cattle fair on Wednesdays, they would remind you of the youth of Pamplona in Spain making mischief with the bulls. As far as the youth of Cabra West was concerned, every beast there was a bull!

Even though they had new houses and a fine new school, poverty followed them. They bore all the signs of hunger. Some were full of fleas and disease. There were up to 2,000 pupils in the school at the beginning of the 1950s and there wasn't room for half of them. I remember the first class I had there – seventy-five pupils crammed into the cloakroom, a terrazzo floor under us with no heat and a couple of children sitting on their own in a front seat – they had hereditary syphilis, rotten teeth and red, sore eyes swollen from the disease. It was not an auspicious start.

A priest would visit every day – 'Toucher Burke', the parish priest, so named because he was always looking for money, and 'Flash Kavanagh' who was famous for saying mass in a quarter of an hour lest he be late for things that interested him more. But, in truth, Flash was held in great affection, as was 'Dash' who was in competition with him for the speed record.

I was lodging with Nelly Reidy in 30 Cabra Road where some of the most famous leaders of the Irish National Teachers' Organisation – Dave Kelliher, Jackie Brosnan, Dave Hanley and Leo McCann – had lodged before they married. She kept only teachers. Once when a niece of hers was visiting from West Cork, the young girl was very anxious to see the schoolmasters. She imagined them as stout, middle aged men in navy suits and hats with gold chains across their bellies. She spent a long time studying them through an opening in the kitchen door when they came down for breakfast. They didn't conform to her vision of schoolmasters – they were young and carelessly dressed. She turned to her aunt and said: 'Auntie Nelly, country teachers is gents!' Nelly was married to the headwaiter in the Metropole and they had no children. Because of his work and because he used be in charge of serving food at the races in the Phoenix Park and Naas, we were well fed on the surplus food he would bring home with him in a pack with Mrs Lawlor's permission from Naas – sandwiches, chickens, salad, trifle and other delicacies. We had no complaints about where they came from!

Down in the city 'Bang Bang' would jump a bus and 'shoot' anybody that stirred with his imaginary gun; and it would take the ex-boxer Billy Burns half an hour to walk from the General Post Office to the Metropole. He was a black man who had fought Jack Johnson twelve times but now was crippled with the effects of his boxing career and he wore carpet slippers on his feet. The city was full of ex-soldiers from the British army who were wounded in the trenches – the Dublin Fusiliers wandering around the city centre, half out of their minds from being gassed, and living in abject poverty.

The literary life of the city was hidden away in pubs like the Palace Bar, the Prince near the Capitol, the Pearl and McDaid's – places frequented by Brendan Behan, Patrick Kavanagh and Myles-na-Gopaleen who received no recognition as poets or writers; they lived boozy, lonely lives but they could liven up any company with their boisterousness. Later on, when poor Behan became famous and wealthy, one of the knockers said to him one day in McDaid's: 'I remember you when your arse was out through your trousers'.

To which Behan replied: 'You don't remember it half as well as I do'.

It was the golden age of theatre. Mícheál Mac Liammóir and Hilton Edwards were at the Gate and for four pence you could see Molière, Shaw or Chekov. The Abbey

Theatre was at the height of its fame and, when I saw Seán O'Casey's plays there for the first time, I knew this was another world, the magical world of the theatre. We went to the Gaiety for the Christmas pantomimes with Jimmy O'Dea and Maureen Potter and you would be still laughing for days afterwards.

When Easter came, it was a relief to leave the city and go home to Ventry where the oats were growing in the cornfields, the fields were covered with daisies, the cowslip was in flower in the shade of the ditches and the birds were making their nests. At the beginning of summer both sides of the road from Annascaul were resplendent with fuchsia and the fresh evening air was like wine with the bouquet of honeysuckle. It was as far as you could get from the nausea of the city and the suffocating smell of diesel. You would see Ventry harbour like a sheet of glass, the sun going down behind Cruach Mhárthan and you would fall asleep to the lullaby of the waves breaking gently on the strand. You were at home.

But nothing lasts forever. My mother died suddenly in 1959; my brother and his wife were raising their family in Ventry and, while they always welcomed me, it was no longer my home. The moment of truth had arrived and I decided to leave the city and return to my native place. I put my roots deep into country soil once again. The days of comfort weren't over because a new chapter of my life opened in Listowel on the banks of the River Feale. Looking west from the garden in front of my house, I could see the mountains I loved so well – Slieve Mish and Caherconree all the way out to Mount Brandon and the country

'Ventry Calling'

of my people. There was no day they didn't remind me of my youth growing up in God's Little Heaven. Farewell to the old life and welcome to the new days that are coming.